# SAP ABAP

## The Ultimate Beginner's Guide

Jameson Garner

# TABLE OF CONTENTS

# SAP ABAP INTRODUCTION

ABAP (Advanced Business Application Programming), is a fourth-generation programming language, used for development and customization purposes in the SAP software. Currently positioned along with Java, as the main language for SAP application server programming, most of the programs are executed under the control of the run-time system. This tutorial explains the key concepts of SAP ABAP.

## Audience

SAP ABAP is a high level language that is primarily used to develop enterprise application for large business and financial institution on SAP platform. This tutorial is designed for those who want to learn the basics of SAP ABAP and advance in the field of software development.

## Prerequisites

You need to have a basic understanding of Java programming and Database technologies like PL/SQL to make the most of this tutorial.

# SAP ABAP - OVERVIEW

ABAP stands for Advanced Business Application Programming, a 4GL (4th generation) language. Currently it is positioned, along with Java, as the main language for SAP application server programming.

Let's start with the high level architecture of SAP system. The 3-tier Client/Server architecture of a typical SAP system is depicted as follows.

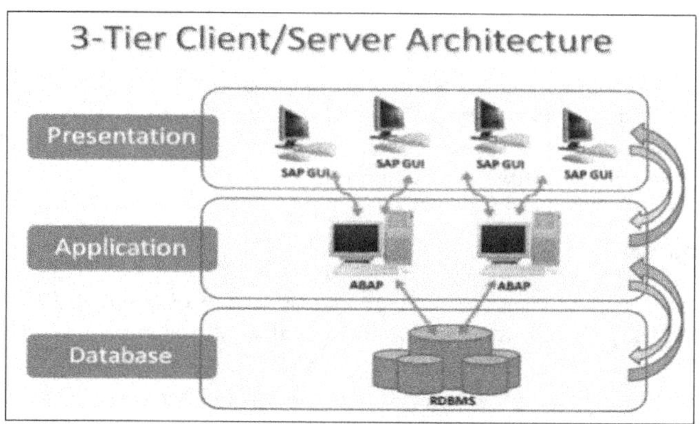



The Presentation layer consists of any input device that can be used to control SAP system. This could be a web browser, a mobile device and so on. All the central processing takes place in Application server. The Application server is not just one system in itself, but it can be multiple instances of the processing system. The server communicates with the Database layer that is usually kept on a separate server, mainly for performance reasons and also for security. Communication happens between each layer of the system, from the Presentation layer to the Database and then back up the chain.

Note − ABAP programs run at the application server level. Technical distribution of software is independent of its physical location. It means basically all three levels can be installed on top of each other on one computer or each level can be installed on a different computer or a server.

ABAP programs reside inside the SAP database. They execute under the control of the runtime system that is a part of the SAP kernel. The run-time system processes all ABAP statements, controlling the flow logic and responding to user events.

So, unlike C++ and Java, ABAP programs are not stored in separate external files. Inside the database, ABAP code exists in two forms −

> ❖ **Source** code that can be viewed and edited with the ABAP workbench tools.

❖ **Generated code**, which is a binary representation. If you are familiar with Java, this generated code is somewhat comparable with Java byte code.

The run-time system can be considered as a virtual machine, just similar to Java virtual machine. A key component of the ABAP run-time system is the database interface that turns database independent statements (Open SQL) into the statements understood by the underlying database (Native SQL). SAP can work with a wide variety of databases and the same ABAP program can run on all of those.

# SAP ABAP - ENVIRONMENT

Reports are a good starting point for familiarizing yourself with general ABAP principles and tools. ABAP reports are used in many areas. In this chapter, we will see how easy it is to write a simple ABAP Report.

## Hello ABAP

Let's get started with the common "Hello World" example.

Each ABAP statement starts with an ABAP keyword and ends with a period. Keywords must be separated by at least one space. It does not matter whether or not you use one or several lines for an ABAP statement.

You need to enter your code using the ABAP Editor that is a part of ABAP Tools delivered with the SAP NetWeaver Application Server ABAP (also known as 'AS ABAP').

'AS ABAP' is an application server with its own database, ABAP run-time environment, and ABAP development tools such as ABAP Editor. The AS ABAP offers a development platform that is independent of hardware, operating system, and database.

## Using the ABAP Editor

**Step 1** − Start the transaction SE38 to navigate to the ABAP Editor (discussed in the next chapter). Let's start creating a report that is one of the many ABAP objects.

**Step 2** − On the initial screen of the editor, specify the name of your report in the input field PROGRAM. You may specify the name as ZHELLO1. The preceding Z is important for the name. Z ensures that your report resides in the customer namespace.

The customer namespace includes all objects with the prefix Y or Z. It is always used when customers or partners create objects (like a report) to differentiate these objects from objects of SAP and to prevent name conflicts with objects.

**Step 3** − You may type the report name in lower case letters, but the editor will change it to upper case. So the names of ABAP objects are 'Not' case sensitive.

**Step 4** − After specifying the name of the report, click the CREATE button. A popup window ABAP: PROGRAM ATTRIBUTES will pop up and you will provide more information about your report.

**Step 5** − Choose "Executable Program" as the report type, enter the title "My First ABAP Report" and then select SAVE to continue. The CREATE OBJECT DIRECTORY ENTRY window will pop up next. Select the button LOCAL OBJECT and the popup will close.

You can complete your first report by entering the WRITE statement below the REPORT statement, so that the complete report contains just two lines as follows −

```
REPORT ZHELLO1.
WRITE 'Hello World'.
```

## Starting the Report

We can use the keyboard (Ctrl + S) or the save icon (right hand side beside the command field) to save the report. ABAP development takes place in AS ABAP.

Starting the report is as simple as saving it. Click the ACTIVATION button (left hand side next to the start icon) and start the report by using the icon DIRECT PROCESSING or the F8 function key. The title "My First ABAP Report" along with the output "Hello World" is displayed as well. Here is the output −

```
My First ABAP Report
Hello World
```

As long as you do not activate a new report or activate a change to an existing report, it is not relevant to their users. This is important in a central development environment where you may work on objects that other developers use in their projects.

## Viewing the Existing Code

If you look at the field Program and double-click on the value ZHELLO1, the ABAP editor will display the code for your report. This is called Forward Navigation. Double clicking on an object's name opens that object in the appropriate tool.SAP ABAP - Screen Navigation

In order to understand SAP ABAP, you need to have basic knowledge of screens like Login, ABAP Editor, Logout and so on. This chapter focuses on screen navigation and the standard toolbar functionality.

## Login Screen

After you log on to SAP server, SAP login screen will prompt for User ID and Password. You need to provide a valid user ID and Password and press Enter (the user id and password is provided by system administrator). Following is the login screen.

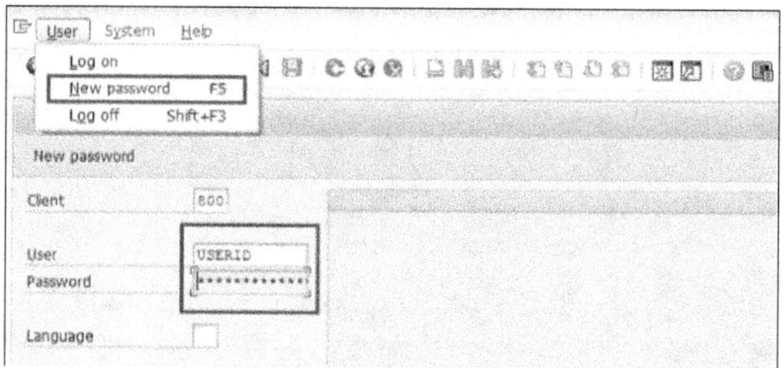

## Toolbar Icon

Following is the SAP screen toolbar.

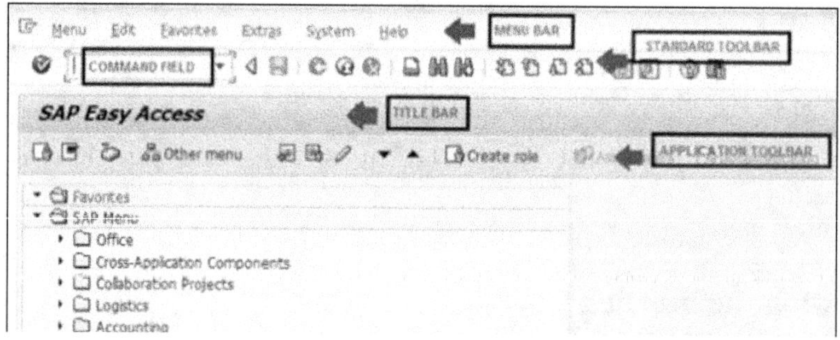


**Menu Bar** – Menu bar is the top line of dialog window.

**Standard Toolbar** – Most standard functions such as Top of Page, End of Page, Page Up, Page Down and Save are available in this toolbar.

**Title Bar** – Title Bar displays the name of the application/business process you are currently in.

**Application Toolbar** – Application specific menu options are available here.

**Command Field** – We can start an application without navigating through the menu transactions and some logical codes are assigned to business processes. Transaction codes are entered in the command field to directly start the application.

## ABAP Editor

You may just start the transaction SE38 (enter SE38 in Command Field) to navigate to the ABAP Editor.

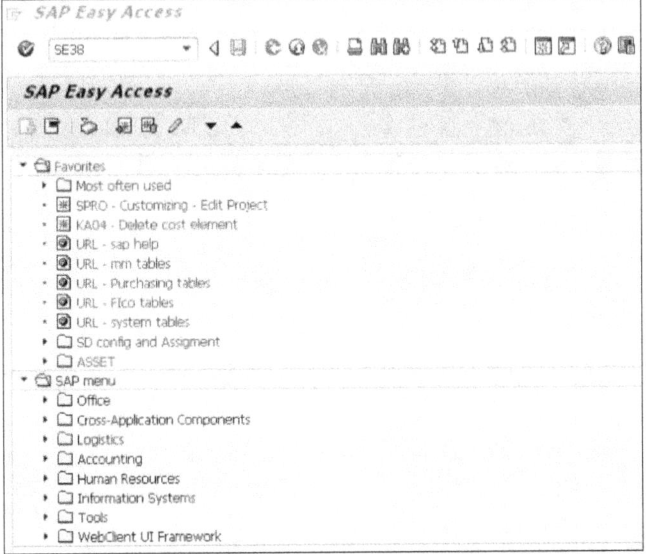

## Standard Keys and Icons

**Exit keys** are used to exit the program/module or to log off. They are also used to go back to the last accessed screen.

Following are the standard exit keys used in SAP as shown in the image.

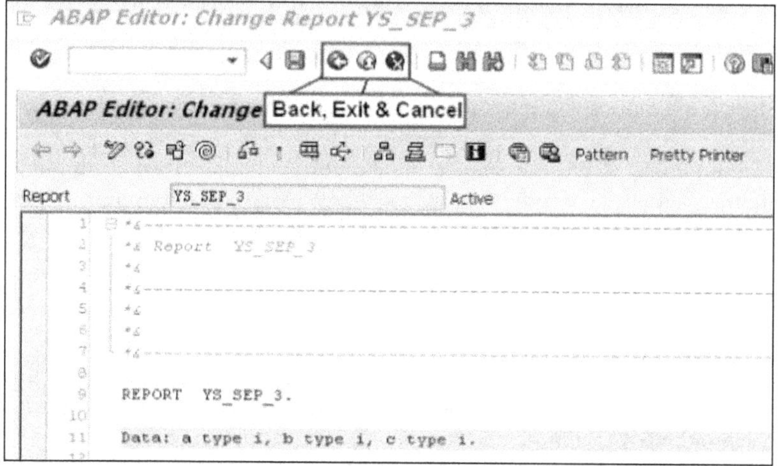



Following are the options for checking, activating and processing the reports.

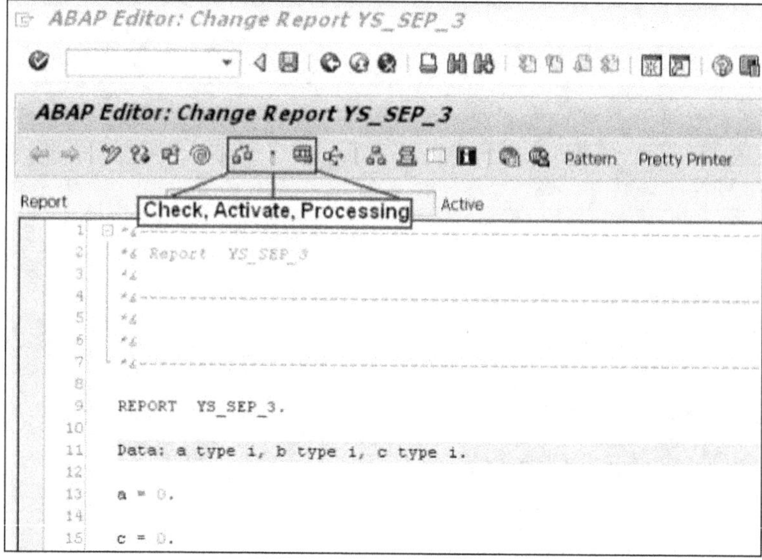



## Log Off

It's always a good practice to Exit from your ABAP Editor or/and logoff from the SAP system after finishing your work.

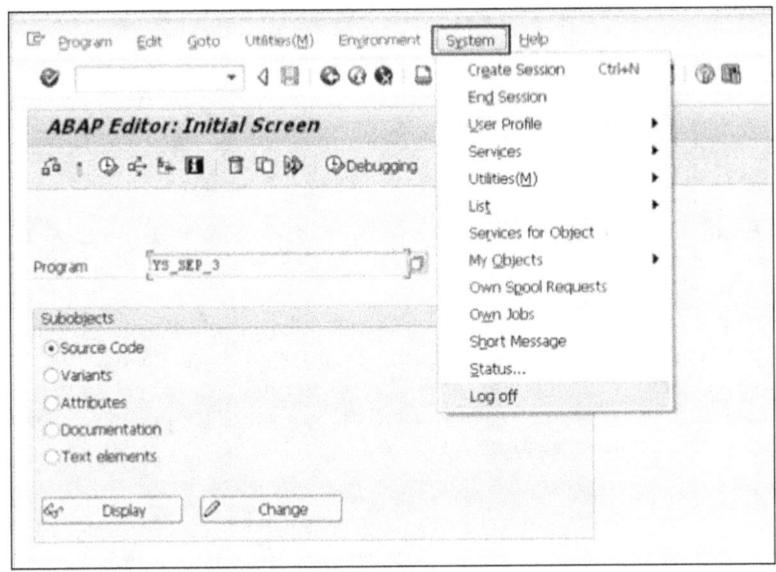


Program   Edit   Goto   Utilities(M)   Environment   System   Help
ABAP Editor: Initial Screen
Debugging
Program   YS_SEP_3
Subobjects
Source Code
Variants
Attributes
Documentation
Text elements
Display   Change
Create Session   Ctrl+N
End Session
User Profile
Services
Utilities(M)
List
Services for Object
My Objects
Own Spool Requests
Own Jobs
Short Message
Status...
Log off

# SAP ABAP - BASIC SYNTAX

## Statements

ABAP source program consists of comments and ABAP statements. Every statement in ABAP begins with a keyword and ends with a period, and ABAP is 'Not' case sensitive.

The first non-comment line in a program begins with the word REPORT. The Report will always be the first line of any executable program created. The statement is followed by the program name which was created previously. The line is then terminated with a full stop.

The syntax is −

```
REPORT [Program_Name].

[Statements…].
```

This allows the statement to take up as many lines in the editor as it needs. For example, the REPORT may look like this −

```
REPORT Z_Test123_01.
```

Statements consist of a command and any variables and options, ending with a period. As long as the period appears at the end of the statement, no problems will arise. It is this period that marks where the statement finishes.

Let's write the code.

On the line below the REPORT statement, just type this statement: Write 'ABAP Tutorial'.

```
REPORT Z_Test123_01.

Write 'This is ABAP Tutorial'.
```

Four things to consider while writing statements −

- ❖ The write statement writes whatever is in quotes to the output window.
- ❖ The ABAP editor converts all text to uppercase except text strings, which are surrounded by single quotation marks.

❖ Unlike some older programming languages, ABAP does not care where a statement begins on a line. You may take advantage of this and improve the readability of your program by using indentation to indicate blocks of code.

❖ ABAP has no restrictions on the layout of statements. That is, multiple statements can be placed on a single line, or a single statement may stretch across multiple lines.

## Colon Notation

Consecutive statements can be chained together if the beginning of each statement is identical. This is done with the colon (:) operator and commas, which are used to terminate the individual statements, much as periods end normal statements.

Following is an example of a program that could save some key stroking −

```
WRITE 'Hello'.
WRITE 'ABAP'.
WRITE 'World'.
```

Using the colon notation, it could be rewritten this way −

```
WRITE: 'Hello',
       'ABAP',
       'World'.
```

Like any other ABAP statement, the layout doesn't matter. This is an equally correct statement −

```
WRITE: 'Hello', 'ABAP', 'World'.
```

## Comments

Inline comments may be declared anywhere in a program by one of the two methods −

❖ Full line comments are indicated by placing an asterisk (*) in the first position of the line, in which case the entire line is considered by the system to be a comment. Comments don't need to be terminated by a period because they may not extend across more than one line −

```
* This is the comment line
```

❖ Partial line comments are indicated by entering a double quote (") after a statement. All text following the double quote is considered by the system to be a comment. You need not terminate partial line comments by a period because they may not extend across more than one line −

```
WRITE 'Hello'. "Here is the partial comment
```

**Note** − Commented code is not capitalized by the ABAP editor.

## Suppressing Blanks

The NO-ZERO command follows the DATA statement. It suppresses all leading zeros of a number field containing blanks. The output is usually easier for the users to read.

Example

```
REPORT Z_Test123_01.

DATA: W_NUR(10) TYPE N.
    MOVE 50 TO W_NUR.
    WRITE W_NUR NO-ZERO.
```

The above code produces the following output −

```
50
```

Note − Without NO-ZERO command, the output is: 0000000050

## Blank Lines

The SKIP command helps in inserting blank lines on the page.

Example

The message command is as follows −

```
WRITE 'This is the 1st line'.
SKIP.
WRITE 'This is the 2nd line'.
```

The above message command produces the following output −

This is the 1st line
This is the 2nd line

We may use the SKIP command to insert multiple blank lines.

SKIP number_of_lines.

The output would be several blank lines defined by the number of lines. The SKIP command can also position the cursor on a desired line on the page.

SKIP TO LINE line_number.

This command is used to dynamically move the cursor up and down the page. Usually, a WRITE statement occurs after this command to put output on that desired line.

## Inserting Lines

The ULINE command automatically inserts a horizontal line across the output. It's also possible to control the position and length of the line. The syntax is pretty simple −

ULINE.

Example

The message command is as follows −

WRITE 'This is Underlined'.
ULINE.

The above code produces the following output −

This is Underlined (and a horizontal line below this).

## Messages

The MESSAGE command displays messages defined by a message ID specified in the REPORT statement at the beginning of the program. The message ID is a 2 character code that defines which set of 1,000 messages the program will access when the MESSAGE command is used.

The messages are numbered from 000 to 999. Associated with each number is a message text up to a maximum of 80 characters. When message number is called, the corresponding text is displayed.

Following are the characters for use with the Message command –

| Message | Type | Consequences |
| --- | --- | --- |
| E | Error | The message appears and the application halts at its current point. If the program is running in background mode, the job is canceled and the message is recorded in the job log. |
| W | Warning | The message appears and the user must press Enter for the application to continue. In background mode, the message is recorded in the job log. |
| I | Information | A pop-up window opens with the message text and the user must press Enter to continue. In background mode, the message is recorded in the job log. |
| A | Abend | This message class cancels the transaction that the user is currently using. |
| S | Success | This provides an informational message at the bottom of the screen. The information displayed is positive in nature and it is just meant for user feedback. The message does not impede the program in any way. |
| X | Abort | This message aborts the program and generates an ABAP short dump. |

Error messages are normally used to stop users from doing things they are not supposed to do. Warning messages are generally used to remind the users of the consequences of their actions. Information messages give the users useful information.

Example

When we create a message for message the ID AB, the MESSAGE command - MESSAGE E011 gives the following output –

EAB011 This report does not support sub-number summarization.

# SAP ABAP - DATA TYPES

While programming in ABAP, we need to use a variety of variables to store various information. Variables are nothing but reserved memory locations to store values. This means that when you create a variable you reserve some space in memory. You may like to store information of various data types like character, integer, floating point, etc. Based on the data type of a variable, the operating system allocates memory and decides what can be stored in the reserved memory.

## Elementary Data Types

ABAP offers the programmer a rich assortment of fixed length as well as variable length data types. Following table lists down ABAP elementary data types −

| Type | Keyword |
|------|---------|
| Byte field | X |
| Text field | C |
| Integer | I |
| Floating point | F |
| Packed number | P |
| Text string | STRING |

Some of the fields and numbers can be modified using one or more names as the following −

- ❖ byte
- ❖ numeric
- ❖ character-like

The following table shows the data type, how much memory it takes to store the value in memory, and the minimum and maximum value that could be stored in such type of variables.

| Type | Typical Length | Typical Range |
|------|----------------|---------------|
| X | 1 byte | Any byte values (00 to FF) |

| Type | Size | Range |
|---|---|---|
| C | 1 character | 1 to 65535 |
| N (numeric text filed) | 1 character | 1 to 65535 |
| D (character-like date) | 8 characters | 8 characters |
| T (character-like time) | 6 characters | 6 characters |
| I | 4 bytes | -2147483648 to 2147483647 |
| F | 8 bytes | 2.2250738585072014E-308 to 1.7976931348623157E+308 positive or negative |
| P | 8 bytes | $[-10^{(2len -1)} +1]$ to $[+10^{(2len -1)} 1]$ (where len = fixed length) |
| STRING | Variable | Any alphanumeric characters |
| XSTRING (byte string) | Variable | Any byte values (00 to FF) |

Example

```
REPORT YR_SEP_12.
DATA text_line TYPE C LENGTH 40.
text_line = 'A Chapter on Data Types'.
Write text_line.

DATA text_string TYPE STRING.
text_string = 'A Program in ABAP'.
Write / text_string.

DATA d_date TYPE D.
d_date = SY-DATUM.
Write / d_date.
```

In this example, we have a character string of type C with a predefined length 40. STRING is a data type that can be used for any character string of variable length (text strings). Type STRING data objects should generally be used for character-like content where fixed length is not important.

The above code produces the following output −

---

A Chapter on Data Types
A Program in ABAP
12092015

---

The DATE type is used for the storage of date information and can store eight digits as shown above.


## Complex and Reference Types

The complex types are classified into Structure types and Table types. In the structure types, elementary types and structures (i.e. structure embedded in a structure) are grouped together. You may consider only the grouping of elementary types. But you must be aware of the availability of nesting of structures.

When the elementary types are grouped together, the data item can be accessed as a grouped data item or the individual elementary type data items (structure fields) can be accessed. The table types are better known as arrays in other programming languages. Arrays can be simple or structure arrays. In ABAP, arrays are called internal tables and they can be declared and operated upon in many ways when compared to other programming languages. The following table shows the parameters according to which internal tables are characterized.

| S.No. | Parameter & Description |
|---|---|
| 1 | Line or row type<br>Row of an internal table can be of elementary, complex or reference type. |
| 2 | Key<br>Specifies a field or a group of fields as a key of an internal table that identifies the table rows. A key contains the fields of elementary types. |
| 3 | Access method<br>Describes how ABAP programs access individual table entries. |

Reference types are used to refer to instances of classes, interfaces, and run-time data items. The ABAP OOP run-time type services (RTTS) enables declaration of data items at run-time.

# SAP ABAP - VARIABLES

Variables are named data objects used to store values within the allotted memory area of a program. As the name suggests, users can change the content of variables with the help of ABAP statements. Each variable in ABAP has a specific type, which determines the size and layout of the variable's memory; the range of values that can be stored within that memory; and the set of operations that can be applied to the variable.

You must declare all variables before they can be used. The basic form of a variable declaration is —

```
DATA <f> TYPE <type> VALUE <val>.
```

Here <f> specifies the name of a variable. The name of the variable can be up to 30 characters long. <type> specifies the type of variable. Any data type with fully specified technical attributes is known as <type>. The <val> specifies the initial value of the of <f> variable. In case you define an elementary fixed-length variable, the DATA statement automatically populates the value of the variable with the type-specific initial value. Other possible values for <val> can be a literal, constant, or an explicit clause, such as Is INITIAL.

Following are valid examples of variable declarations.

```
DATA d1(2) TYPE C.
DATA d2 LIKE d1.
DATA minimum_value TYPE I VALUE 10.
```

In the above code snippet, d1 is a variable of C type, d2 is a variable of d1 type, and minimum_value is a variable of ABAP integer type I.

This chapter will explain various variable types available in ABAP. There are three kinds of variables in ABAP —

- ❖ Static Variables
- ❖ Reference Variables
- ❖ System Variables

## Static Variables

- ❖ Static variables are declared in subroutines, function modules, and static methods.
- ❖ The lifetime is linked to the context of the declaration.
- ❖ With 'CLASS-DATA' statement, you can declare variables within the classes.

- ❖ The 'PARAMETERS' statement can be used to declare the elementary data objects that are linked to input fields on a selection screen.
- ❖ You can also declare the internal tables that are linked to input fields on a selection screen by using 'SELECT-OPTIONS' statement.

Following are the conventions used while naming a variable −

- ❖ You cannot use special characters such as "t" and "," to name variables.
- ❖ The name of the predefined data objects can't be changed.
- ❖ The name of the variable can't be the same as any ABAP keyword or clause.
- ❖ The name of the variables must convey the meaning of the variable without the need for further comments.
- ❖ Hyphens are reserved to represent the components of structures. Therefore, you are supposed to avoid hyphens in variable names.
- ❖ The underscore character can be used to separate compound words.

This program shows how to declare a variable using the PARAMETERS statement −

```
REPORT ZTest123_01.
PARAMETERS: NAME(10) TYPE C,
CLASS TYPE I,
SCORE TYPE P DECIMALS 2,
CONNECT TYPE MARA-MATNR.
```

Here, NAME represents a parameter of 10 characters, CLASS specifies a parameter of integer type with the default size in bytes, SCORE represents a packed type parameter with values up to two decimal places, and CONNECT refers to the MARA-MATNF type of ABAP Dictionary.

The above code produces the following output −

| NAME | |
| CLASS | |
| SCORE | |
| CONNECT | |

## Reference Variables

The syntax for declaring reference variables is −

```
DATA <ref> TYPE REF TO <type> VALUE IS INITIAL.
```

- ❖ REF TO addition declares a reference variable ref.
- ❖ The specification after REF TO specifies the static type of the reference variable.
- ❖ The static type restricts the set of objects to which <ref> can refer.
- ❖ The dynamic type of reference variable is the data type or class to which it currently refers.
- ❖ The static type is always more general or the same as the dynamic type.
- ❖ The TYPE addition is used to create a bound reference type and as a start value, and only IS INITIAL can be specified after the VALUE addition.

Example

```
CLASS C1 DEFINITION.
PUBLIC SECTION.
DATA Bl TYPE I VALUE 1.
ENDCLASS. DATA: Oref TYPE REF TO C1 ,
Dref1 LIKE REF TO Oref,
Dref2 TYPE REF TO I .
CREATE OBJECT Oref.
GET REFERENCE OF Oref INTO Dref1.
CREATE DATA Dref2.
Dref2→* = Dref1→*→Bl.
```

- ❖ In the above code snippet, an object reference Oref and two data reference variables Dref1 and Dref2 are declared.
- ❖ Both data reference variables are fully typed and can be dereferenced using the dereferencing operator →* at operand positions.

## System Variables

- ❖ ABAP system variables are accessible from all ABAP programs.
- ❖ These fields are actually filled by the run-time environment.
- ❖ The values in these fields indicate the state of the system at any given point of time.
- ❖ You can find the complete list of system variables in the SYST table in SAP.
- ❖ Individual fields of the SYST structure can be accessed by using either "SYST-" or "SY-".

## Example

```
REPORT Z_Test123_01.

WRITE:/'SY-ABCDE', SY-ABCDE,
   /'SY-DATUM', SY-DATUM,
```

```
        /'SY-DBSYS', SY-DBSYS,
        /'SY-HOST ', SY-HOST,
        /'SY-LANGU', SY-LANGU,
        /'SY-MANDT', SY-MANDT,
        /'SY-OPSYS', SY-OPSYS,
        /'SY-SAPRL', SY-SAPRL,
        /'SY-SYSID', SY-SYSID,
        /'SY-TCODE', SY-TCODE,
        /'SY-UNAME', SY-UNAME,
        /'SY-UZEIT', SY-UZEIT.
```

The above code produces the following output −

```
SY-ABCDE ABCDEFGHIJKLMNOPQRSTUVWXYZ
SY-DATUM 12.09.2015
SY-DBSYS ORACLE
SY-HOST sapserver
SY-LANGU EN
SY-MANDT 800
SY-OPSYS Windows NT
SY-SAPRL 700
SY-SYSID DMO
SY-TCODE SE38
SY-UNAME SAPUSER
SY-UZEIT 14:25:48
```

# SAP ABAP - CONSTANTS & LITERALS

Literals are unnamed data objects that you create within the source code of a program. They are fully defined by their value. You can't change the value of a literal. Constants are named data objects created statically by using declarative statements. A constant is declared by assigning a value to it that is stored in the program's memory area. The value assigned to a constant can't be changed during the execution of the program. These fixed values can also be considered as literals. There are two types of literals − numeric and character.

## Numeric Literals

Number literals are sequences of digits which can have a prefixed sign. In number literals, there are no decimal separators and no notation with mantissa and exponent.

Following are some examples of numeric literals −

```
183.
-97.
+326.
```

## Character Literals

Character literals are sequences of alphanumeric characters in the source code of an ABAP program enclosed in single quotation marks. Character literals enclosed in quotation marks have the predefined ABAP type C and are described as text field literals. Literals enclosed in "back quotes" have the ABAP type STRING and are described as string literals. The field length is defined by the number of characters.

**Note** − In text field literals, trailing blanks are ignored, but in string literals they are taken into account.

Following are some examples of character literals.

Text field literals

```
REPORT YR_SEP_12.
Write 'Tutorials Point'.
Write / 'ABAP Tutorial'.
```

String field literals

```
REPORT YR_SEP_12.
Write `Tutorials Point `.
Write / `ABAP Tutorial `.
```

The output is same in both the above cases −

```
Tutorials Point
ABAP Tutorial
```

**Note** − When we try to change the value of the constant, a syntax or run-time error may occur. Constants that you declare in the declaration part of a class or an interface belong to the static attributes of that class or interface.

## CONSTANTS Statement

We can declare the named data objects with the help of CONSTANTS statement.

Following is the syntax −

```
CONSTANTS <f> TYPE <type> VALUE <val>.
```

The CONSTANTS statement is similar to the DATA statement.

<f> specifies a name for the constant. TYPE <type> represents a constant named <f>, which inherits the same technical attributes as the existing data type <type>. VALUE <val> assigns an initial value to the declared constant name <f>.

**Note** − We should use the VALUE clause in the CONSTANTS statement. The clause 'VALUE' is used to assign an initial value to the constant during its declaration.

We have 3 types of constants such as elementary, complex and reference constants. The following statement shows how to define constants by using the CONSTANTS statement −

```
REPORT YR_SEP_12.
CONSTANTS PQR TYPE P DECIMALS 4 VALUE '1.2356'.
Write: / 'The value of PQR is:', PQR.
```

The output is −

The value of PQR is: 1.2356

Here it refers to elementary data type and is known as elementary constant.

Following is an example for complex constants −

```
BEGIN OF EMPLOYEE,
Name(25) TYPE C VALUE 'Management Team',
Organization(40) TYPE C VALUE 'Tutorials Point Ltd',
Place(10) TYPE C VALUE 'India',
END OF EMPLOYEE.
```

In the above code snippet, EMPLOYEE is a complex constant that is composed of the Name, Organization and Place fields.

The following statement declares a constant reference −

```
CONSTANTS null_pointer TYPE REF TO object VALUE IS INITIAL.
```

We can use the constant reference in comparisons or we may pass it on to procedures.

ABAP provides a rich set of operators to manipulate variables. All ABAP operators are classified into four categories −

- ❖ Arithmetic Operators
- ❖ Comparison Operators
- ❖ Bitwise Operators
- ❖ Character String Operators

## Arithmetic Operators

Arithmetic operators are used in mathematical expressions in the same way that they are used in algebra. The following list describes arithmetic operators. Assume integer variable A holds 20 and variable B holds 40.

| S.No. | Arithmetic Operator & Description |
|---|---|
| 1 | + (Addition)<br>Adds values on either side of the operator. Example: A + B will give 60. |
| 2 | − (Subtraction)<br>Subtracts right hand operand from left hand operand. Example: A − B will give -20. |
| 3 | * (Multiplication)<br>Multiplies values on either side of the operator. Example: A * B will give 800. |
| 4 | / (Division)<br>Divides left hand operand by right hand operand. Example: B / A will give 2. |
| 5 | MOD (Modulus)<br>Divides left hand operand by right hand operand and returns the remainder. Example: B MOD A will give 0. |

Example

```
REPORT YS_SEP_08.
DATA: A TYPE I VALUE 150,
B TYPE I VALUE 50,
Result TYPE I.
```

```
Result = A / B.
WRITE / Result.
```

The above code produces the following output −

```
3
```

## Comparison Operators

Let's discuss the various types of comparison operators for different operands.

| S.No. | Comparison Operator & Description |
| --- | --- |
| 1 | = (equality test). Alternate form is EQ.<br>Checks if the values of two operands are equal or not, if yes then condition becomes true. Example (A = B) is not true. |
| 2 | <> (Inequality test). Alternate form is NE.<br>Checks if the values of two operands are equal or not. If the values are not equal then the condition becomes true. Example (A <> B) is true. |
| 3 | > (Greater than test). Alternate form is GT.<br>Checks if the value of left operand is greater than the value of right operand. If yes then condition becomes true. Example (A > B) is not true. |
| 4 | < (Less than test). Alternate form is LT.<br>Checks if the value of left operand is less than the value of right operand. If yes, then condition becomes true. Example (A < B) is true. |
| 5 | >= (Greater than or equals) Alternate form is GE.<br>Checks if the value of left operand is greater than or equal to the value of right Operand. If yes, then condition becomes true. Example (A >= B) is not true. |
| 6 | <= (Less than or equals test). Alternate form is LE.<br>Checks if the value of left operand is less than or equal to the value of right operand. If yes, then condition becomes true. Example (A <= B) is true. |
| 7 | a1 BETWEEN a2 AND a3 (Interval test)<br>Checks whether a1 lies in between a2 and a3 (inclusive). If yes, then the condition becomes true. Example (A BETWEEN B AND C) is |

true.

| 8 | IS INITIAL |
| | The condition becomes true if the contents of the variable have not changed and it has been automatically assigned its initial value. Example (A IS INITIAL) is not true |

| 9 | IS NOT INITIAL |
| | The condition becomes true if the contents of the variable have changed. Example (A IS NOT INITIAL) is true. |

**Note** − If the data type or length of the variables does not match then automatic conversion is performed. Automatic type adjustment is performed for either one or both of the values while comparing two values of different data types. The conversion type is decided by the data type and the preference order of the data type.

Following is the order of preference −

- ❖ If one field is of type I, then the other is converted to type I.
- ❖ If one field is of type P, then the other is converted to type P.
- ❖ If one field is of type D, then the other is converted to type D. But C and N types are not converted and they are compared directly. Similar is the case with type T.
- ❖ If one field is of type N and the other is of type C or X, both the fields are converted to type P.
- ❖ If one field is of type C and the other is of type X, the X type is converted to type C.

## Example 1

```
REPORT YS_SEP_08.

DATA: A TYPE I VALUE 115,
   B TYPE I VALUE 119.
   IF A LT B.
   WRITE: / 'A is less than B'.
   ENDIF
```

The above code produces the following output −

```
A is less than B
```

# Example 2

```
REPORT YS_SEP_08.

DATA: A TYPE I.
    IF A IS INITIAL.
    WRITE: / 'A is assigned'.
    ENDIF.
```

The above code produces the following output −

```
A is assigned.
```

## Bitwise Operators

ABAP also provides a series of bitwise logical operators that can be used to build Boolean algebraic expressions. The bitwise operators can be combined in complex expressions using parentheses and so on.

| S.No. | Bitwise Operator & Description |
|---|---|
| 1 | **BIT-NOT**<br>Unary operator that flips all the bits in a hexadecimal number to the opposite value. For instance, applying this operator to a hexadecimal number having the bit level value 10101010 (e.g. 'AA') would give 01010101. |
| 2 | **BIT-AND**<br>This binary operator compares each field bit by bit using the Boolean AND operator. |
| 3 | **BIT-XOR**<br>Binary operator that compares each field bit by bit using the Boolean XOR (exclusive OR) operator. |
| 4 | **BIT-OR**<br>Binary operator that compares each field bit by bit using the Boolean OR operator. |

For example, following is the truth table that shows the values generated when applying the Boolean AND, OR, or XOR operators against the two bit values contained in field A and field B.

| Field A | Field B | AND | OR | XOR |
| --- | --- | --- | --- | --- |
| 0 | 0 | 0 | 0 | 0 |
| 0 | 1 | 0 | 1 | 1 |
| 1 | 0 | 0 | 1 | 1 |
| 1 | 1 | 1 | 1 | 0 |

Character String Operators

Following is a list of character string operators −

| S.No. | Character String Operator & Description |
| --- | --- |
| 1 | **CO (Contains Only)**<br>Checks whether A is solely composed of the characters in B. |
| 2 | **CN (Not Contains ONLY)**<br>Checks whether A contains characters that are not in B. |
| 3 | **CA (Contains ANY)**<br>Checks whether A contains at least one character of B. |
| 4 | **NA (NOT Contains Any)**<br>Checks whether A does not contain any character of B. |
| 5 | **CS (Contains a String)**<br>Checks whether A contains the character string B. |
| 6 | **NS (NOT Contains a String)**<br>Checks whether A does not contain the character string B. |
| 7 | **CP (Contains a Pattern)**<br>It checks whether A contains the pattern in B. |
| 8 | **NP (NOT Contains a Pattern)**<br>It checks whether A does not contain the pattern in B. |

Example

```
REPORT YS_SEP_08.
DATA: P(10) TYPE C VALUE 'APPLE',
```

```
Q(10) TYPE C VALUE 'CHAIR'.
IF P CA Q.

WRITE: / 'P contains at least one character of Q'.
ENDIF.
```

The above code produces the following output −

```
P contains at least one character of Q.
```

There may be a situation when you need to execute a block of code several number of times. In general, statements are executed sequentially: The first statement in a function is executed first, followed by the second, and so on.

Programming languages provide various control structures that allow for more complicated execution paths. A loop statement allows us to execute a statement or group of statements multiple times and following is the general form of a loop statement in most of the programming languages.

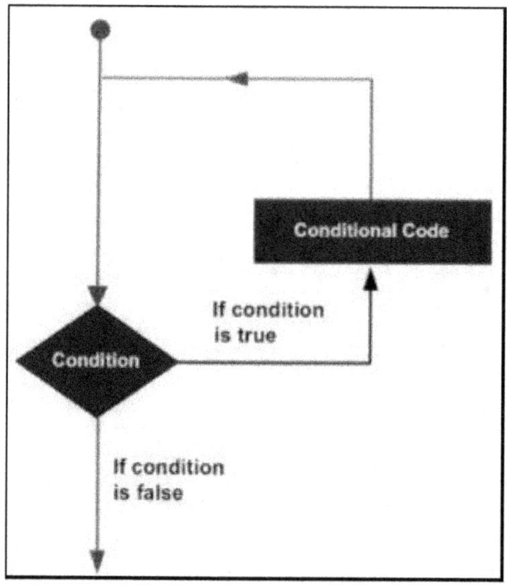


ABAP programming language provides the following types of loop to handle looping requirements.

| S.No. | Loop Type & Description |
| --- | --- |
| 1 | **WHILE loop** <br> Repeats a statement or group of statements when a given condition is true. It tests the condition before executing the loop body. |
| 2 | **Do loop** <br> The DO statement is useful for repeating particular task a specific number of times. |
| 3 | **Nested loop** |

You may use one or more loops inside any another WHILE or DO loop.

## Loop Control Statements

Loop control statements change execution from its normal sequence. ABAP includes control statements that allow loops to be ended prematurely. It supports the following control statements.

| S.No. | Control Statement & Description |
|---|---|
| 1 | **CONTINUE**<br>Causes the loop to skip the remainder of its body and starts the next loop pass. |
| 2 | **CHECK**<br>If the condition is false, then the remaining statements after the CHECK are just ignored and the system starts the next loop pass. |
| 3 | **EXIT**<br>Terminates the loop entirely and transfers execution to the statement immediately following the loop. |

# SAP ABAP - DECISIONS

Decision making structures have one or more conditions to be evaluated or tested by the program, along with a statement or statements that are to be executed, if the condition is determined to be true, and optionally, other statements to be executed, if the condition is determined to be false.

Following is the general form of a typical decision-making structure found in most of the programming languages −

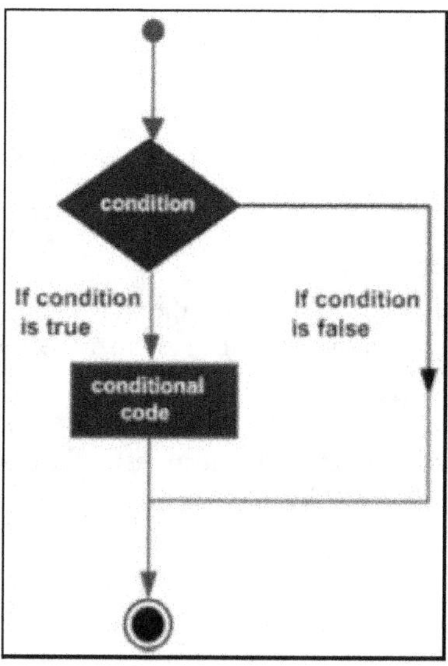



ABAP programming language provides the following types of decision-making statements.

| S.No. | Statement & Description |
|-------|-------------------------|
| 1 | **IF Statement**<br>An IF statement consists of a logical expression followed by one or more statements. |
| 2 | **IF.. Else Statement**<br>An IF statement can be followed by an optional ELSE statement that executes when the expression is false. |
| 3 | **Nested IF Statement**<br>You may use one IF or ELSEIF statement inside another IF or ELSEIF statement. |

4       **CASE Control Statement**

CASE statement is used when we need to compare two or more fields or variables.

# SAP ABAP - STRINGS

**Strings**, which are widely used in ABAP programming, are a sequence of characters.

We use data type C variables for holding alphanumeric characters, with a minimum of 1 character and a maximum of 65,535 characters. By default, these are aligned to the left.

## Creating Strings

The following declaration and initialization creates a string consisting of the word 'Hello'. The size of the string is exactly the number of characters in the word 'Hello'.

```
Data my_Char(5) VALUE 'Hello'.
```

Following program is an example of creating strings.

```
REPORT YT_SEP_15.
DATA my_Char(5) VALUE 'Hello'.
Write my_Char.
```

The above code produces the following output −

```
Hello
```

## String Length

In order to find the length of character strings, we can use STRLEN statement. The STRLEN () function returns the number of characters contained in the string.

Example

```
REPORT YT_SEP_15.
DATA: title_1(10) VALUE 'Tutorials',
    length_1 TYPE I.

length_1 = STRLEN( title_1 ).
Write: / 'The Length of the Title is:', length_1.
```

The above code produces the following output −

The Length of the Title is: 9

ABAP supports a wide range of statements that manipulate strings.

| S.No. | Statement & Purpose |
|---|---|
| 1 | CONCATENATE<br>Two strings are joined to form a third string. |
| 2 | CONDENSE<br>This statement deletes the space characters. |
| 3 | STRLEN<br>Used to find the length of a field. |
| 4 | REPLACE<br>Used to make replacements in characters. |
| 5 | SEARCH<br>To run searches in character strings. |
| 6 | SHIFT<br>Used to move the contents of a string left or right. |
| 7 | SPLIT<br>Used to split the contents of a field into two or more fields. |

The following example makes use of some of the above mentioned statements −

# Example

```
REPORT YT_SEP_15.
DATA: title_1(10) VALUE 'Tutorials',
    title_2(10) VALUE 'Point',
    spaced_title(30) VALUE 'Tutorials  Point  Limited',
    sep,
    dest1(30),
    dest2(30).

CONCATENATE title_1 title_2 INTO dest1.
Write: / 'Concatenation:', dest1.
```

CONCATENATE title_1 title_2 INTO dest2 SEPARATED BY sep.
Write: / 'Concatenation with Space:', dest2.

CONDENSE spaced_title.
Write: / 'Condense with Gaps:', spaced_title.

CONDENSE spaced_title NO-GAPS.
Write: / 'Condense with No Gaps:', spaced_title.

The above code produces the following output −

Concatenation: TutorialsPoint
Concatenation with Space: Tutorials Point
Condense with Gaps: Tutorials Point Limited
Condense with No Gaps: TutorialsPointLimited

**Note −**

- ❖ In case of Concatenation, the 'sep' inserts a space in between the fields.
- ❖ The CONDENSE statement removes blank spaces between the fields, but leaving only 1 character's space.
- ❖ 'NO-GAPS' is an optional addition to the CONDENSE statement that removes all spaces.

# SAP ABAP - DATE & TIME

ABAP implicitly references the Gregorian calendar, valid across most of the world. We can convert the output to country specific calendars. A date is a time specified to a precise day, week or month with respect to a calendar. A time is specified to a precise second or minute with respect to a day. ABAP always saves time in 24-hour format. The output can have a country specific format. Dates and time are usually interpreted as local dates that are valid in the current time zone.

ABAP provides two built-in types to work with dates and time −

- ❖ D data type
- ❖ T data type

Following is the basic format −

```
DATA: date TYPE D,
      time TYPE T.

DATA: year TYPE I,
month TYPE I,
day TYPE I,
hour TYPE I,
minute TYPE I,
second TYPE I.
```

Both of these types are fixed-length character types that have the form YYYYMMDD and HHMMSS, respectively.

## Timestamps

In addition to these built-in types, the other two types TIMESTAMP and TIMESTAMPL are being used in many standard application tables to store a timestamp in the UTC format. Following table shows the basic date and time types available in ABAP.

| S.No. | Data Type & Description |
|---|---|
| 1 | D<br>A built-in fixed-length date type of the form YYYYMMDD. For example, the value 20100913 represents the date September 13, 2010. |
| 2 | T<br>A built-in fixed-length time type of the form HHMMSS. For example, |

the value 102305 represents time 10:23:05 AM.

3       TIMESTAMP (Type P – Length 8 No decimals)
This type is used to represent short timestamps in YYYYMMDDhhmmss form. For instance, the value 20100913102305 represents the date September 13, 2010 at 10:23:05 AM.

4       TIMESTAMPL (Type P - Length 11 Decimals 7)
TIMESTAMPL represents long timestamps in YYYYMMDDhhmmss,mmmuuun form. Here the additional digits 'mmmuuun' represent the fractions of a second.

## Current Date and Time

The following code snippets retrieve the current system date and time.

```
REPORT YR_SEP_15.
DATA: date_1 TYPE D.

date_1 = SY-DATUM.
Write: / 'Present Date is:', date_1 DD/MM/YYYY.

date_1 = date_1 + 06.
Write: / 'Date after 6 Days is:', date_1 DD/MM/YYYY.
```

The above code produces the following output −

```
Present Date is: 21.09.2015
Date after 6 Days is: 27.09.2015
```

The variable date_1 is assigned the value of the current system date SY-DATUM. Next, we increment the date value by 6. In terms of a date calculation in ABAP, this implies that we're increasing the day component of the date object by 6 days. The ABAP runtime environment is smart enough to roll over the date value whenever it reaches the end of a month.

Time calculations work similar to date calculations. The following code increments the current system time by 75 seconds using basic time arithmetic.

```
REPORT YR_SEP_15.
DATA: time_1 TYPE T.
    time_1 = SY-UZEIT.
```

```
Write /(60) time_1 USING EDIT MASK
'Now the Time is: __:__:__'.
time_1 = time_1 + 75.

Write /(60) time_1 USING EDIT MASK
'A Minute and a Quarter from Now, it is: __:__:__'.
```

The above code produces the following output −

```
Now the Time is 11:45:05
A Minute and a Quarter from Now, it is: 11:46:20
```

## Working with Timestamps

You can retrieve the current system time and store it in a timestamp variable using GET TIME STAMP as shown in the following code. The GET TIME STAMP statement stores the timestamp in a long-hand or a short-hand format according to the type of the timestamp data object used. Timestamp value is encoded using the UTC standard.

```
REPORT YR_SEP_12.
DATA: stamp_1 TYPE TIMESTAMP,

stamp_2 TYPE TIMESTAMPL.
GET TIME STAMP FIELD stamp_1.
Write: / 'The short time stamp is:', stamp_1

TIME ZONE SY-ZONLO.
GET TIME STAMP FIELD stamp_2.
Write: / 'The long time stamp is:', stamp_2
TIME ZONE SY-ZONLO.
```

The above code produces the following output −

```
The short time stamp is: 18.09.2015 11:19:40
The long time stamp is: 18.09.2015 11:19:40,9370000
```

In the above example, we are displaying the timestamp using the TIME ZONE addition of the WRITE statement. This addition formats the output of the timestamp according to the rules for the time zone specified. The system field SY-ZONLO is used to display the local time zone configured in the user's preferences.

# SAP ABAP - FORMATTING DATA

ABAP offers various types of formatting options to format the output of programs. For example, you can create a list that includes various items in different colors or formatting styles.

The WRITE statement is a formatting statement used to display data on a screen. There are different formatting options for the WRITE statement. The syntax of the WRITE statement is −

WRITE <format> <f> <options>.

In this syntax, <format> represents the output format specification, which can be a forward slash (/) that indicates the display of the output starting from a new line. In addition to the forward slash, the format specification includes a column number and column length. For example, the WRITE/04 (6) statement shows that a new line begins with column 4 and the column length is 6, whereas the WRITE 20 statement shows the current line with column 20. The parameter <f> represents a data variable or numbered text.

The following table describes various clauses used for formatting −

| S.No. | Clause & Description |
| --- | --- |
| 1 | **LEFT-JUSTIFIED**<br>Specifies that the output is left-justified. |
| 2 | **CENTERED**<br>Denotes that the output is centered. |
| 3 | **RIGHT-JUSTIFIED**<br>Specifies that the output is right-justified. |
| 4 | **UNDER <g>**<br>The output starts directly under the field <g>. |
| 5 | **NO-GAP**<br>Specifies that the blank after field <f> is rejected. |
| 6 | **USING EDIT MASK <m>**<br>Denotes the specification of the format template <m>. Using No EDIT Mask: This specifies that the format template specified in the ABAP Dictionary is deactivated. |

| 7 | **NO-ZERO** |
| | If a field contains only zeroes, then they are replaced by blanks. |

Following are the formatting options for Numeric Type fields −

| S.No. | Clause & Description |
| --- | --- |
| 1 | **NO-SIGN** <br> Specifies that no leading sign is displayed on the screen. |
| 2 | **EXPONENT <e>** <br> Specifies that in type F (the floating point fields), the exponent is defined in <e>. |
| 3 | **ROUND <r>** <br> The type P fields (packed numeric data types) are first multiplied by $10^{**}(-r)$ and then rounded off to an integer value. |
| 4 | **CURRENCY <c>** <br> Denotes that the formatting is done according to the currency <c> value that is stored in the TCURX database table. |
| 5 | **UNIT <u>** <br> Specifies that the number of decimal places is fixed according to the <u> unit as specified in the T006 database table for type P. |
| 6 | **DECIMALS <d>** <br> Specifies that the number of digits <d> must be displayed after the decimal point. |

For instance, the following table shows different formatting options for the date fields −

| Formatting Option | Example |
| --- | --- |
| DD/MM/YY | 13/01/15 |
| MM/DD/YY | 01/13/15 |
| DD/MM/YYYY | 13/01/2015 |
| MM/DD/YYYY | 01/13/2015 |
| DDMMYY | 130115 |

| MMDDYY | 011315 |
| YYMMDD | 150113 |

Here, DD stands for the date in two figures, MM stands for the month in two figures, YY stands for the year in two figures, and YYYY stands for the year in four figures.

Let's take a look at an example of ABAP code that implements some of the above formatting options −

```
REPORT ZTest123_01.

DATA: n(9) TYPE C VALUE 'Tutorials',
m(5) TYPE C VALUE 'Point'.

WRITE: n, m.
WRITE: / n,
/ m UNDER n.

WRITE: / n NO-GAP, m.
DATA time TYPE T VALUE '112538'.

WRITE: / time,
/(8) time Using EDIT MASK '__:__:__'.
```

The above code produces the following output −

```
Tutorials Point
Tutorials
Point
TutorialsPoint
112538
11:25:38
```

# SAP ABAP - EXCEPTION HANDLING

An exception is a problem that arises during the execution of a program. When an exception occurs the normal flow of the program is disrupted and the program application terminates abnormally, which is not recommended, therefore these exceptions are to be handled.

Exceptions provide a way to transfer control from one part of a program to another. ABAP exception handling is built upon three keywords − RAISE, TRY, CATCH and CLEANUP. Assuming a block will raise an exception, a method catches an exception using a combination of the TRY and CATCH keywords. A TRY - CATCH block is placed around the code that might generate an exception. Following is the syntax for using TRY − CATCH −

```
TRY.
Try Block <Code that raises an exception>

CATCH
Catch Block <exception handler M>
. . .
. . .
. . .
CATCH
Catch Block <exception handler R>

CLEANUP.
   Cleanup block <to restore consistent state>

ENDTRY.
```

**RAISE** − Exceptions are raised to indicate that some exceptional situation has occurred. Usually, an exception handler tries to repair the error or find an alternative solution.

**TRY** − The TRY block contains the application coding whose exceptions are to be handled. This statement block is processed sequentially. It can contain further control structures and calls of procedures or other ABAP programs. It is followed by one or more catch blocks.

**CATCH** − A program catches an exception with an exception handler at the place in a program where you want to handle the problem. The CATCH keyword indicates the catching of an exception.

**CLEANUP** – The statements of the CLEANUP block are executed whenever an exception occurs in a TRY block that is not caught by the handler of the same TRY - ENDTRY construct. Within the CLEANUP clause, the system can restore an object to a consistent state or release external resources. That is, cleanup work can be executed for the context of the TRY block.

## Raising Exceptions

Exceptions can be raised at any point in a method, a function module, a subroutine, and so on. There are two ways an exception can be raised –

❖ Exceptions raised by ABAP runtime system.

For instance Y = 1 / 0. This will result in a run time error of type CX_SY_ZERODIVIDE.

❖ Exceptions raised by programmer.

Raise and create an exception object simultaneously. Raise an exception with an exception object that already exists in the first scenario. The syntax is: RAISE EXCEPTION exep.

## Catching Exceptions

Handlers are used to catch exceptions.

Let's take a look at a code snippet –

```
DATA: result TYPE P LENGTH 8 DECIMALS 2,
exref TYPE REF TO CX_ROOT,
msgtxt TYPE STRING.
PARAMETERS: Num1 TYPE I, Num2 TYPE I.
TRY.
result = Num1 / Num2.
CATCH CX_SY_ZERODIVIDE INTO exref.
msgtxt = exref ->GET_TEXT().

CATCH CX_SY_CONVERSION_NO_NUMBER INTO exref.
msgtxt = exref->GET_TEXT().
```

In the above code snippet, we are trying to divide Num1 by Num2 to get the result in a float type variable.

Two types of exceptions could be generated.

- ❖ Number conversion error.
- ❖ Divide by zero exception. Handlers catch
  CX_SY_CONVERSION_NO_NUMBER exception and also the
  CX_SY_ZERODIVIDE exception. Here the GET_TEXT( ) method of
  the exception class is used to get the description of the exception.

## Attributes of Exceptions

Here are the five attributes and methods of exceptions −

| S.No. | Attribute & Description |
|---|---|
| 1 | **Textid**<br>Used to define different texts for exceptions and also affects the result of the method get_text. |
| 2 | **Previous**<br>This attribute can store the original exception that allows you to build a chain of exceptions. |
| 3 | **get_text**<br>This returns the textual representation as a string as per the system language of the exception. |
| 4 | **get_longtext**<br>This returns the long variant of the textual representation of the exception as a string. |
| 5 | **get_source_position**<br>Gives the program name and line number reached where the exception was raised. |

Example

```
REPORT ZExceptionsDemo.
PARAMETERS Num_1 TYPE I.

DATA res_1 TYPE P DECIMALS 2.
DATA orf_1 TYPE REF TO CX_ROOT.
DATA txt_1 TYPE STRING.

start-of-selection.
Write: / 'Square Root and Division with:', Num_1.
write: /.
```

```
TRY.
IF ABS( Num_1 ) > 150.
RAISE EXCEPTION TYPE CX_DEMO_ABS_TOO_LARGE.
ENDIF.

TRY.
res_1 = SQRT( Num_1 ).
Write: / 'Result of square root:', res_1.
res_1 = 1 / Num_1.

Write: / 'Result of division:', res_1.
CATCH CX_SY_ZERODIVIDE INTO orf_1.
txt_1 = orf_1→GET_TEXT( ).
CLEANUP.
CLEAR res_1.
ENDTRY.

CATCH CX_SY_ARITHMETIC_ERROR INTO orf_1.
txt_1 = orf_1→GET_TEXT( ).

CATCH CX_ROOT INTO orf_1.
txt_1 = orf_1→GET_TEXT( ).
ENDTRY.
IF NOT txt_1 IS INITIAL.
Write / txt_1.
ENDIF.
Write: / 'Final Result is:', res_1.
```

In this example, if the number is greater than 150, the exception
CX_DEMO_ABS_TOO_LARGE is raised. The above code produces the
following output for the number 160.

```
Square Root and Division with: 160
The absolute value of number is too high
Final Result is:  0.00
```

# SAP ABAP - DICTIONARY

As you are aware, SQL can be divided into two parts −

- ❖ DML (Data Manipulation Language)
- ❖ DDL (Data Definition Language)

DML part consists of query and update commands such as SELECT, INSERT, UPDATE, DELETE, etc. and ABAP programs handle the DML part of SQL. DDL part consists of commands such as CREATE TABLE, CREATE INDEX, DROP TABLE, ALTER TABLE, etc. and ABAP Dictionary handles the DDL part of SQL.

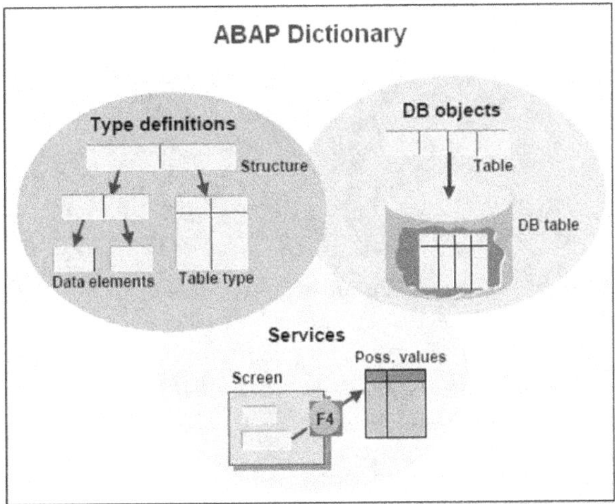


ABAP Dictionary can be viewed as metadata (i.e. data about data) that resides in the SAP database along with the metadata maintained by the database. The Dictionary is used to create and manage data definitions and to create Tables, Data Elements, Domains, Views and Types.

## Basic Types in ABAP Dictionary

The basic types in ABAP Dictionary are as follows −

- ❖ **Data elements** describe an elementary type by defining the data type, length and possibly decimal places.
- ❖ **Structures** with components that can have any type.
- ❖ **Table types** describe the structure of an internal table.

Various objects in the Dictionary environment can be referenced in ABAP programs. The Dictionary is known as the global area. The objects in the Dictionary are global to all ABAP programs and the data in ABAP programs can be declared by reference to these Dictionary global objects.

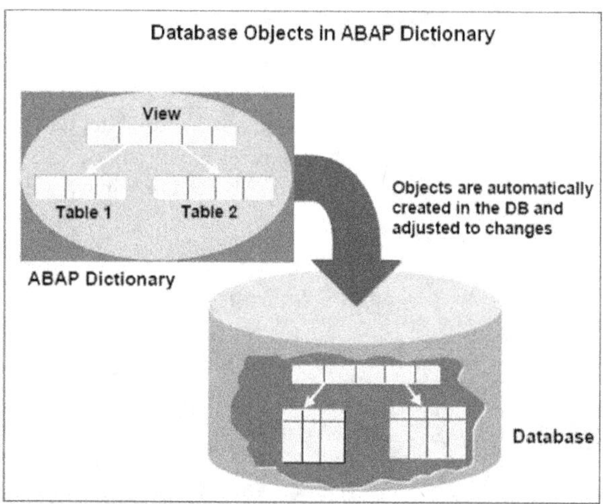


The Dictionary supports the definition of user-defined types and these types are used in ABAP programs. They also define the structure of database objects such as tables, views and indexes. These objects are created automatically in the underlying database in their Dictionary definitions when the objects are activated. The Dictionary also provides editing tools like Search Help and locking tool like Lock Objects.

## Dictionary Tasks

ABAP Dictionary achieves the following −

- ❖ Enforces data integrity.
- ❖ Manages data definitions without redundancy.
- ❖ Integrates tightly with rest of the ABAP development workbench.

Example

Any complex user-defined type can be built from the 3 basic types in the Dictionary. Customer data is stored in a structure 'Customer' with the components Name, Address and Telephone as depicted in the following image. Name is also a structure with components, First name and Last name. Both of these components are elementary because their type is defined by a data element.

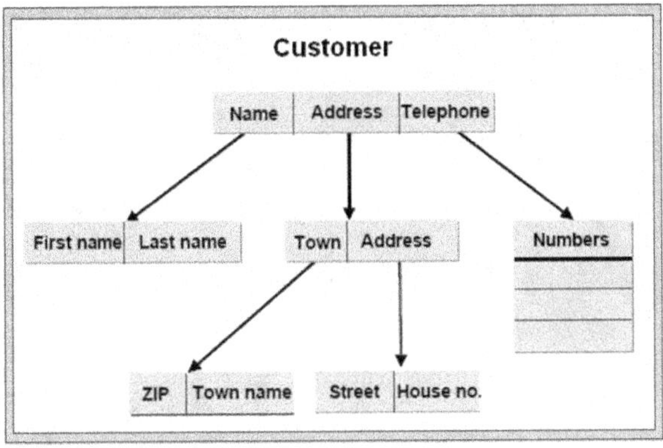


The type of component Address is defined by a structure whose components are also structures, and the Telephone component is defined by a table type because a customer can have more than one telephone number. Types are used in ABAP programs and also to define the types of interface parameters of function modules.

The three basic objects for defining data in the ABAP Dictionary are Domains, Data elements and Tables. The domain is used for the technical definition of a table field such as field type and length, and the data element is used for the semantic definition (short description). A data element describes the meaning of a domain in a certain business context. It contains primarily the field help and the field labels in the screen.

The domain is assigned to the data element, which in turn is assigned to the table fields or structure fields. For instance, the MATNR domain (CHAR material number) is assigned to data elements such as MATNR_N, MATNN and MATNR_D, and these are assigned to many table fields and structure fields.

## Creating Domains

Before you create a new domain, check whether any existing domains have the same technical specifications required in your table field. If so, we are supposed to use that existing domain. Let's discuss the procedure for creating the domain.

**Step 1** – Go to Transaction SE11.

**Step 2** – Select the radio button for Domain in the initial screen of the ABAP Dictionary, and enter the name of the domain as shown in the following screenshot. Click the CREATE button. You may create domains under the customer namespaces, and the name of the object always starts with 'Z' or 'Y'.

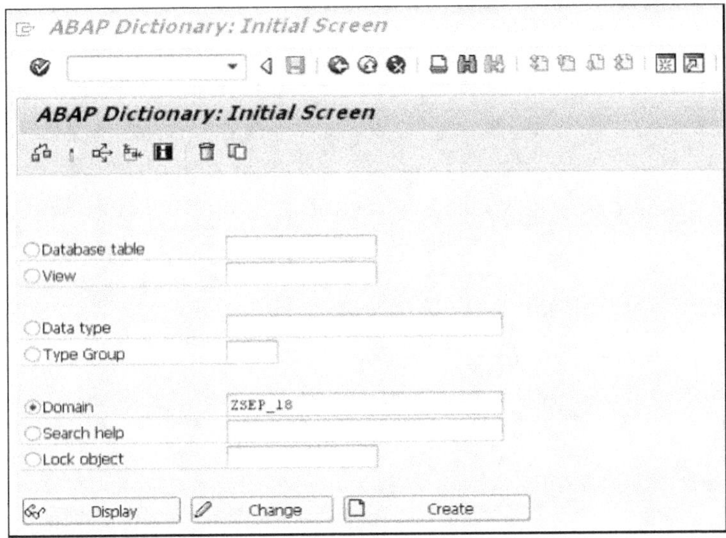



**Step 3** – Enter the description in the short text field of the maintenance screen of the domain. In this case, it is "Customer Domain". Note – You cannot enter any other attribute until you have entered this attribute.

**Step 4** – Enter the Data Type, No. of Characters, and Decimal Places in the Format block of the Definition tab. Press the key on Output Length and it proposes and displays the output length. If you overwrite the proposed output length, you may see a warning while activating the domain. You may fill in the Convers. Routine, Sign and Lower Case fields if required. But these are always optional attributes.

**Step 5** – Select the Value Range tab. If the domain is restricted to having only fixed values then enter the fixed values or intervals. Define the value table if the system has to propose this table as a check table while defining a foreign key for the fields referring to this domain. But all these are optional attributes.

Dictionary: Change Domain

| Domain | ZSEP_18 | New(Revised) |
| Short Description | Customer Domain | |

Properties | Definition | Value Range

Format

| Data Type | NUMC | Character string with only digits |
| No. Characters | 8 | |
| Decimal Places | 0 | |

Output Characteristics

| Output Length | 8 |
| Convers. Routine | |
| ☐ Sign | |
| ☐ Lower Case | |

**Step 6** – Save your changes. The Create Object Directory Entry pop-up appears and asks for a package. You may enter the package name in which you are working. If you do not have any package then you may create it in the Object Navigator or you can save your domain using the Local Object button.

**Step 7** – Activate your domain. Click on the Activate icon (matchstick icon) or press CTRL + F3 to activate the domain. A pop-up window appears, listing the 2 currently inactive objects as shown in the following snapshot –

Transportable Objects | Local objects

Object name

| D.. Object | Obj. name |
| DOMA | ZSEP_18 |
| DOMA | Z_SEP_21 |

**Step 8** – At this point, the top entry labeled 'DOMA' with the name ZSEP_18 is to be activated. As this is highlighted, click the green tick button. This window disappears and the status bar will display the message 'Object activated'.

If error messages or warnings occurred when you activated the domain, the activation log is displayed automatically. The activation log displays information about activation flow. You can also call the activation log with Utilities(M) → Activation log.

# SAP ABAP - DATA ELEMENTS

Data elements describe the individual fields in the ABAP Data Dictionary. They are the smallest indivisible units of the complex types, and they are used to define the type of table field, structure component or row type of a table. Information about the meaning of a table field and also information about editing the corresponding screen field could be assigned to a data element. This information is automatically available to all the screen fields that refer to the data element. Data elements describe either elementary types or reference types.

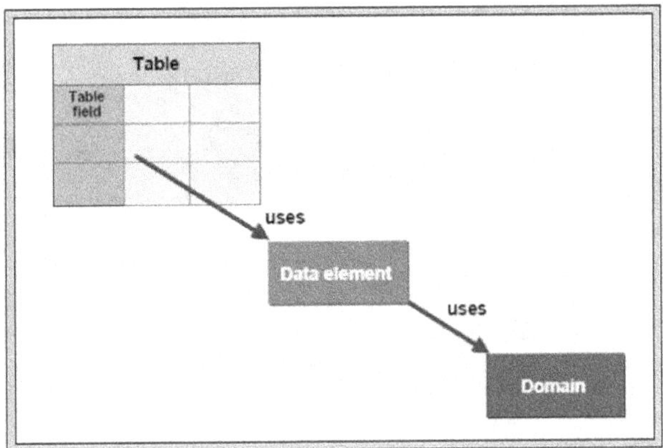


## Creating Data Elements

Before creating a new data element, you need to check whether any existing data elements have the same semantic specifications required in your table field. If so, you may use that existing data element. You can assign the data element with a predefined type, domain, or reference type.

Following is the procedure for creating the data element −

**Step 1** − Go to Transaction SE11.

**Step 2** − Select the radio button for Data type in the initial screen of the ABAP Dictionary, and enter the name of the data element as shown below.

**Step 3** − Click the CREATE button. You may create data elements under the customer namespaces, and the name of the object always starts with 'Z' or 'Y'.

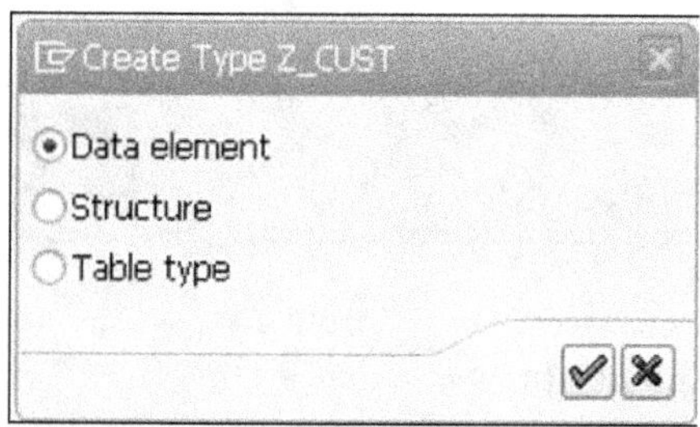

**Step 4** − Check the Data element radio button on the CREATE TYPE pop-up that appears with three radio buttons.

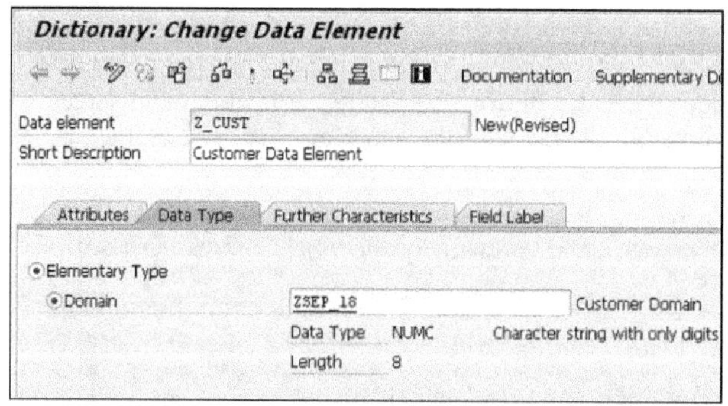

**Step 5** − Click the green checkmark icon. You are directed to the maintenance screen of the data element.

**Step 6** − Enter the description in the short text field of the maintenance screen of the data element. In this case, it is "Customer Data Element". Note − You cannot enter any other attribute until you have entered this attribute.

**Step 7** − Assign the data element with the type. You can create an elementary data element by checking elementary type or a reference data element by checking Reference type. You can assign a data element to a Domain or Predefined Type within Elementary Type and with Name of Reference Type or Reference to Predefined Type within Reference Type.

**Step 8** − Enter the fields for short text, medium text, long text, and heading in the Field Label tab. You can press Enter and the length is automatically generated for these labels.

**Step 9** − Save your changes. The Create Object Directory Entry pop-up appears and asks for a package. You may enter the package name in which you are working. If you do not have any package then you may create it in the Object Navigator or you can save your data element using the Local Object button.

**Step 10** − Activate your data element. Click the Activate icon (matchstick icon) or press CTRL + F3 to activate the data element. A pop-up window appears, listing the 2 currently inactive objects as shown in the following screenshot.

**Step 11** − At this point, the top entry labeled 'DTEL' with the name Z_CUST is to be activated. As this is highlighted, click the green tick button. This window disappears and the status bar will display the message 'Object activated'.

If error messages or warnings occurred when you activated the data element, the activation log is displayed automatically. The activation log displays information about activation flow. You can also call the activation log with Utilities(M) $\rightarrow$ Activation log.

# SAP ABAP - TABLES

Tables can be defined independent of the database in ABAP Dictionary. When a table is activated in ABAP Dictionary, similar copy of its fields is created in the database as well. The tables defined in ABAP Dictionary are translated automatically into the format that is compatible with the database because the definition of the table depends on the database used by the SAP system.

A table can contain one or more fields, each defined with its data type and length. The large amount of data stored in a table is distributed among the several fields defined in the table.

## Types of Table Fields

A table consists of many fields, and each field contains many elements. The following table lists the different elements of table fields –

| S.No. | Elements & Description |
|---|---|
| 1 | **Field name**<br>This is the name given to a field that can contain a maximum of 16 characters. The field name may be composed of digits, letters, and underscores. It must begin with a letter. |
| 2 | **Key flag**<br>Determines whether or not a field belongs to a key field. |
| 3 | **Field type**<br>Assigns a data type to a field. |
| 4 | **Field length**<br>The number of characters that can be entered in a field. |
| 5 | **Decimal places**<br>Defines the number of digits permissible after the decimal point. This element is used only for numeric data types. |
| 6 | **Short text**<br>Describes the meaning of the corresponding field. |

# Creating Tables in ABAP Dictionary

**Step 1** – Go to transaction SE11, select the 'Database table' radio button, and enter a name for the table to be created. In our case, we have entered the name ZCUSTOMERS1. Click the Create button. The Dictionary: Maintain Table screen appears. Here the 'Delivery and Maintenance' tab is selected by default.

**Step 2** – Enter an explanatory short text in the Short Description field.

**Step 3** – Click the Search Help icon beside the Delivery Class field. Select 'A [Application table (master and transaction data)]' option.

**Step 4** – Select the 'Display/Maintenance Allowed' option from the 'Data Browser/Table view Maintenance' drop-down menu. The Dictionary: Maintenance Table screen appears.

| Transp. Table | ZCUSTOMERS1 | New(Revised) |
|---|---|---|
| Short Description | Customers Table | |

| Attributes | Delivery and Maintenance | Fields | Entry help/check | Curr |
|---|---|---|---|---|

| Delivery Class | | A Application table (master and transaction |
|---|---|---|
| Data Browser/Table View Maint. | | Display/Maintenance Allowed |

**Step 5** – Select the Fields tab. The screen containing the options related to the Fields tab appears.

**Step 6** – Enter the names of table fields in the Field column. A field name may contain letters, digits, and underscores, but it must always begin with a letter and must not be longer than 16 characters.

The fields that are to be created must also have data elements because they take the attributes, such as data type, length, decimal places, and short text, from the defined data element.

**Step 7** – Select the Key column if you want the field to be a part of the table key. Let's create fields such as CLIENT, CUSTOMER, NAME, TITLE and DOB.

**Step 8** – The first field is an important one and it identifies the client which the records are associated with. Enter 'Client' as the Field and 'MANDT' as the Data Element. The system automatically fills in the Data Type, Length, Decimals and Short Description. The 'Client' field is made a key field by checking the 'Key' box.

**Step 9** – The next field is 'Customer'. Check the box to make it a key field and enter the new Data Element 'ZCUSTNUM'. Click the Save button.

**Step 10** – As the Data Element 'ZCUSTNUM' doesn't yet exist, it has to be created. Doubleclick the new Data Element and the 'Create Data Element' window appears. Answer 'Yes' to this and a 'Maintain Data Element' window appears.

**Step 11** – Enter 'Customer Number' in the Short Description area. The Elementary data type called 'Domain' should be defined for the new Data element. So enter 'ZCUSTD1', double-click it and agree to save the changes made. Choose 'Yes' to create the domain and type into the 'Short Description' box a description of the domain.



The 'Definition' tab opens automatically. The first field is 'Data Type'.

**Step 12** – Click inside the box and select 'NUMC' type from the drop-down menu. Enter the number 8 in the 'No. of characters' field (a maximum of 8 characters) and enter 0 in 'Decimal places' area. The Output length of 8 must be selected and then press Enter. The 'NUMC' field's description must re-appear, confirming that this is a valid entry.

**Step 13** – Click Save button and Activate the object.

**Step 14** – Press F3 to return to the 'Maintain/Change Data Element' screen. Create four Field labels as shown in the following snapshot. After this, Save and Activate the element.

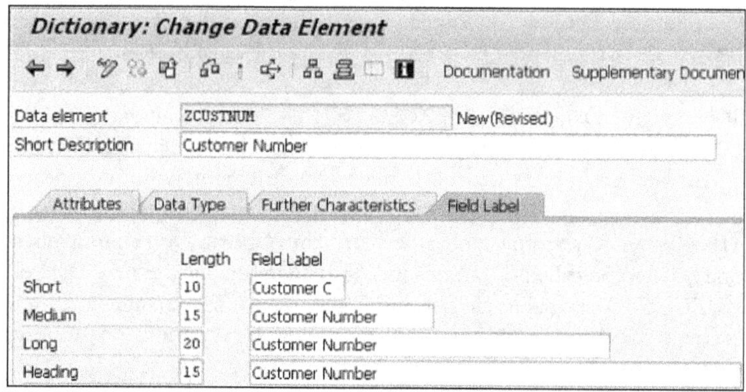



**Step 15** − Press the back button to return to the table maintenance screen. The Customer column has the correct Data Type, Length, Decimals and Short Description. This indicates the successful creation of a Data element and also the Domain used.

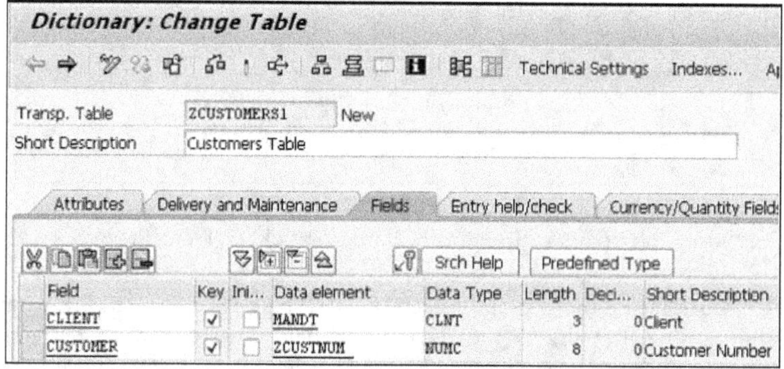



Similarly, we need to create three additional fields such as NAME, TITLE and DOB.

**Step 16** − Select 'Technical settings' from the toolbar. Choose APPL0 for the 'Data class' and the first size category 0 for the 'Size' category' field. In case of buffering options, 'Buffering not allowed' has to be selected.

**Step 17** − Click Save. Go back to the table and Activate it. The following screen appears.

**Dictionary: Display Table**

Technical Settings    Indexes...    App

| Transp. Table | ZCUSTOMERS1 | Active |
| Short Description | Customers Table | |

Attributes   Delivery and Maintenance   Fields   Entry help/check   Currency/Quantity Fields

Srch Help   Predefined Type

| Field | Key | Ini... | Data element | Data Type | Length | Deci... | Short Description |
|---|---|---|---|---|---|---|---|
| CLIENT | ✓ | | MANDT | CLNT | 3 | 0 | Client |
| CUSTOMER | ✓ | | ZCUSTNUM | NUMC | 8 | 0 | Customer Number |
| NAME | | | ZCUSTNAME | CHAR | 40 | 0 | Name Data Element |
| TITLE | | | ZTITLE1 | CHAR | 15 | 0 | Title Data Element |
| DOB | | | ZDOB1 | DATS | 8 | 0 | DOB Data Element |

The table 'ZCUSTOMERS1' is activated.

Structure is a data object that is made up of components of any data type stored one after the other in the memory.

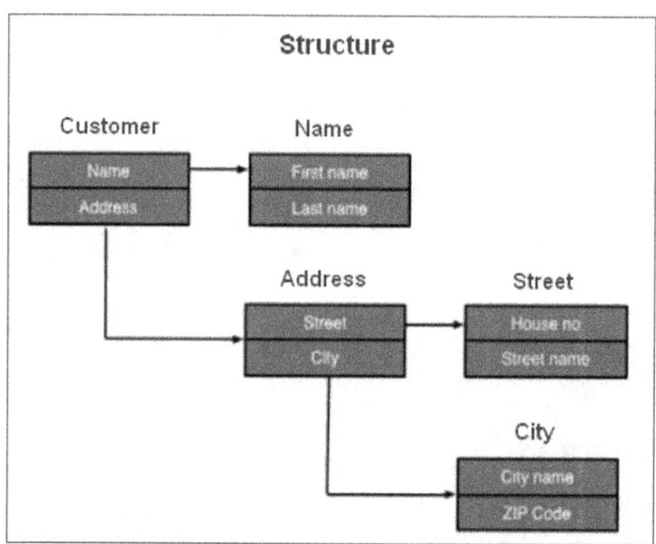



Structures are useful for painting screen fields, and for manipulating data that has a consistent format defined by a discrete number of fields.

A structure may have only a single record at run-time, but a table can have many records.

## Creating a Structure

**Step 1** – Go to transaction SE11.

**Step 2** – Click on the 'Data type' option on the screen. Enter the name 'ZSTR_CUSTOMER1' and click on Create button.

**Step 3** – Select the option 'Structure' in the next screen and press Enter. You can see 'Maintain / Change Structure' wizard.

**Step 4** – Enter the Short Description as shown in the following snapshot.

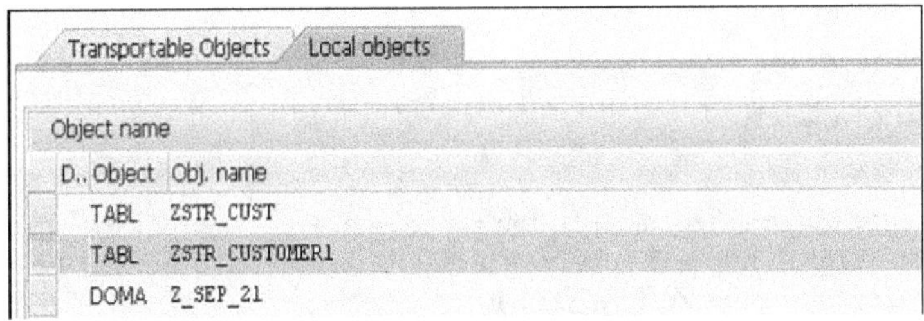

**Step 5** – Enter the Component (Field Name) and Component Type (Data Element).

Note &minu; Here the component names start with Z as per the SAP recommendation. Let's use data elements that we have already created in the database table.

**Step 6** – You need to Save, Check and Activate after providing all the components and component types.

The following screen appears –

**Step 7** – As this 'ZSTR_CUSTOMER1' is highlighted, click the green tick button. This window disappears and the status bar will display the message 'Active'.

The structure is now activated as shown in the following snapshot –

A View acts like a database table only. But it will not occupy storage space. A view acts similar to a virtual table - a table that does not have any physical existence. A view is created by combining the data of one or more tables containing information about an application object. Using views, you can represent a subset of the data contained in a table or you can join multiple tables into a single virtual table.

Data related to an application object is distributed among multiple tables by using database views. They use the inner join condition to join the data of different tables. A maintenance view is used to display and modify the data stored in an application object. Every maintenance view has a maintenance status associated with it.

We use projection view to mask unwanted fields and display only relevant fields in a table. Projection views must be defined over a single transparent table. A projection view contains exactly one table. We can't define selection conditions for projection views.

## Creating a View

**Step 1** − Select the View radio button on the initial screen of ABAP Dictionary. Enter the name of the view to be created and then click Create button. We entered the name of the view as ZVIEW_TEST.

**Step 2** − Select the projection view radio button while choosing view type and click Copy button. The 'Dictionary: Change View' screen appears.

**Step 3** − Enter a short description in the Short Description field and the name of the table to be used in the Basis Table field as shown in the following snapshot.

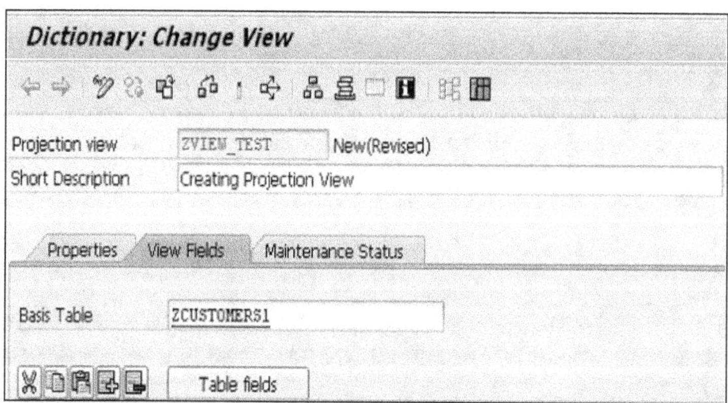

**Step 4** − Click the 'Table fields' button to include the fields of ZCUSTOMERS1 table in the projection view.

**Step 5** − The Field Selection from Table ZCUSTOMERS1 screen appears. Select the fields that you wish to include in the projection view as shown in the following snapshot.

**Step 6** − After clicking the Copy button, all the selected fields for the projection view are displayed on the 'Dictionary: Change View' screen.

**Step 7** − Select Maintenance Status tab to define an access method. Choose read-only radio button and 'Display/Maintenance Allowed with Restrictions' option from the dropdown menu of 'Data Browser/Table View Maintenance'.

**Step 8** − Save and Activate it. In the 'Dictionary: Change View' screen select Utilities(M) > Contents to display the selection screen for ZVIEW_TEST.

**Step 9** − Click the Execute icon. The output of the projection view appears as shown in the following screenshot.

Data Browser: Table ZVIEW_TEST Select Entries          4

Table:              ZVIEW_TEST
Displayed Fields:    3 of   3          Fixed Columns:            2

| | Client | Customer Number | Name |
|---|---|---|---|
| | 800 | 00100001 | MARK |
| | 800 | 00100002 | JAMES |
| | 800 | 00100003 | AURIELE |
| | 800 | 00100004 | STEPHEN |

The table ZCUSTOMERS1 consists of 5 fields. Here the displayed fields are 3 (Client, Customer Number and Name) with 4 entries. Customer numbers are from 100001 to 100004 with appropriate names.

# SAP ABAP - SEARCH HELP

Search Help, another repository object of ABAP Dictionary, is used to display all the possible values for a field in the form of a list. This list is also known as a hit list. You can select the values that are to be entered in the fields from this hit list instead of manually entering the value, which is tedious and error prone.

## Creating Search Help

**Step 1** − Go to transaction SE11. Select the radio button for Search help. Enter the name of the search help to be created. Let's enter the name ZSRCH1. Click on the Create button.

**Step 2** − The system will prompt for the search help type to be created. Select the Elementary search help, which is default. The screen to create elementary search help as shown in the following screenshot appears.

**Step 3** − In the selection method, we need to indicate whether our source of data is a table or a view. In our case it happens to be a table. The table is ZCUSTOMERS1. It is selected from a selection list.

**Step 4** − After the selection method is entered, the next field is the Dialog type. This controls the appearance of the restrictive dialog box. There is a drop-down list with three options. Let's select the option 'Display values immediately'.

**Step 5** − Next is the parameter area. For each Search help parameter or field, these column fields have to be entered as per the requirements.

> ❖ Search help parameter − This is a field from the source of data. The fields from the table are listed in the selection list. The fields participating in the search help would be entered, one field in each row. Let's include the two

fields CUSTOMER and NAME. How these two fields participate is indicated in the rest of the columns.

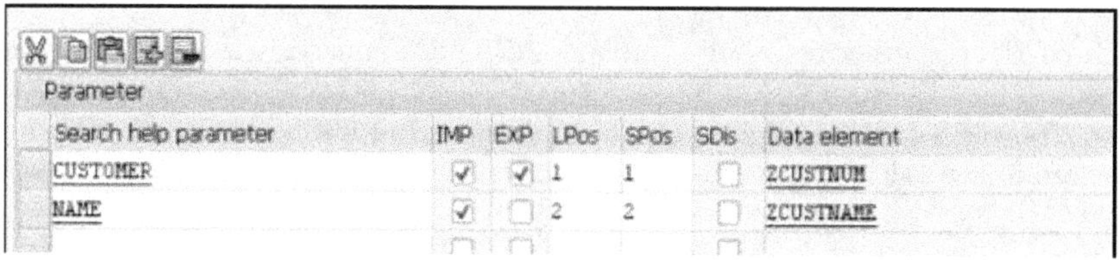

- ❖ Import − This field is a checkbox for indicating whether a Search help parameter is an import parameter. The export or import is with reference to the search help.
- ❖ Export − This field is a checkbox for indicating whether a Search help parameter is an export parameter. The export will be transfer of field values from the selection list to screen fields.
- ❖ LPos − Its value controls the physical position of Search help parameter or field in the selection list. If you enter a value 1, the field will appear in the first position in the selection list and so on.
- ❖ SPos − It controls the physical position of Search Help parameter or field in the restrictive dialog box. If you enter a value of 1, the field will appear in the first position in the restrictive dialog box and so on.
- ❖ Data element − Every Search Help parameter or field by default is assigned a data element that was assigned to it in the source of data (Table or View). This data element name appears in display mode.

**Step 6** − Perform a consistency check and activate the search help. Press F8 to execute. The 'Test Search Help ZSRCH1' screen appears as shown in the following screenshot.

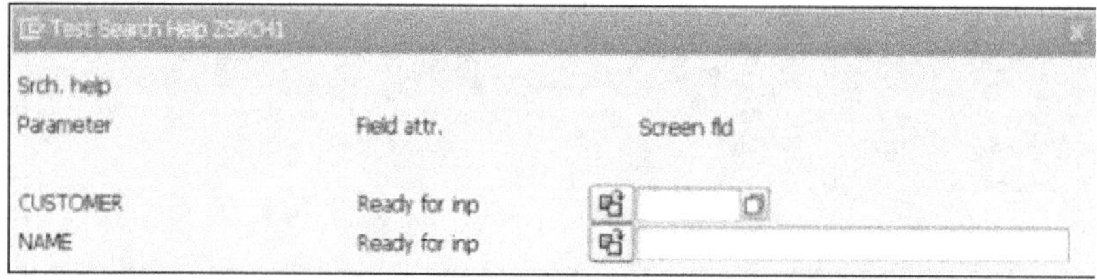

**Step 7** − Let's enter the number 100004 in the CUSTOMER's 'Ready for inp' screen field. Press Enter.

The customer number, 100004, and the name 'STEPHEN' is displayed.

# SAP ABAP - LOCK OBJECTS

Lock Object is a feature offered by ABAP Dictionary that is used to synchronize access to the same data by more than one program. Data records are accessed with the help of specific programs. Lock objects are used in SAP to avoid the inconsistency when data is inserted into or changed in the database. Tables whose data records are to be locked must be defined in a Lock Object, along with their key fields.

## Lock Mechanism

Following are the two main functions accomplished with the lock mechanism −

- ❖ A program can communicate with other programs about data records that it is just reading or changing.
- ❖ A program can prevent itself from reading data that has just been changed by another program.

A lock request is first generated by the program. Then this request goes to the Enqueue server and the lock is created in the lock table. The Enqueue server sets the lock and the program is finally ready to access data.

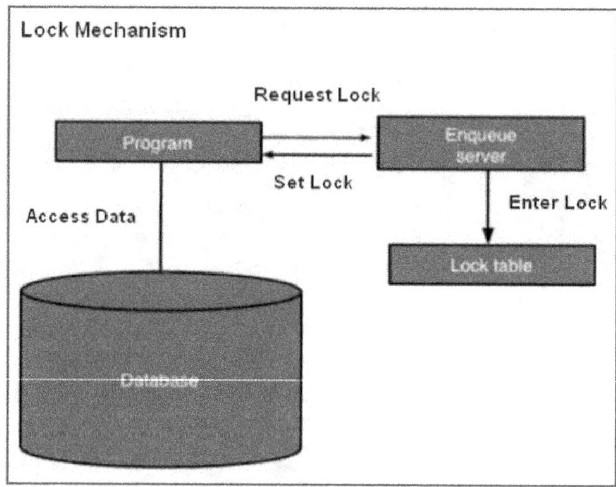


## Creating Lock Objects

**Step 1** − Go to transaction SE11. The following screen opens.

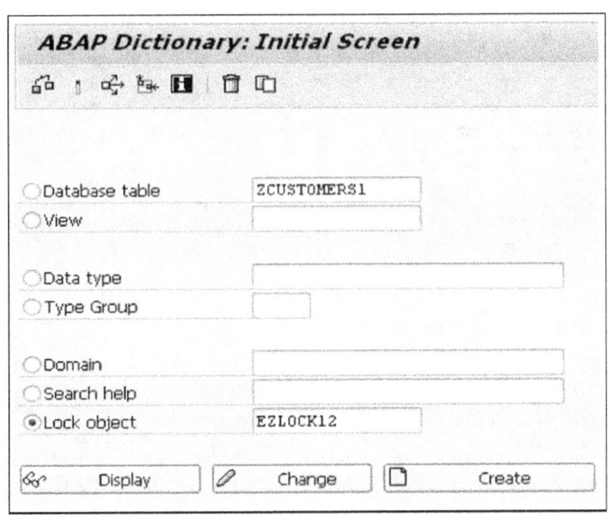



**Step 2** − Click 'Lock Object' radio button. Enter the name of lock object starting with E and click the Create button. Here we use EZLOCK12.

**Step 3** − Enter the short description field and click on Tables tab.

**Step 4** − Enter the table name in Name field and select the lock mode as Write Lock.

**Step 5** − Click on Lock parameter tab, the following screen will appear.

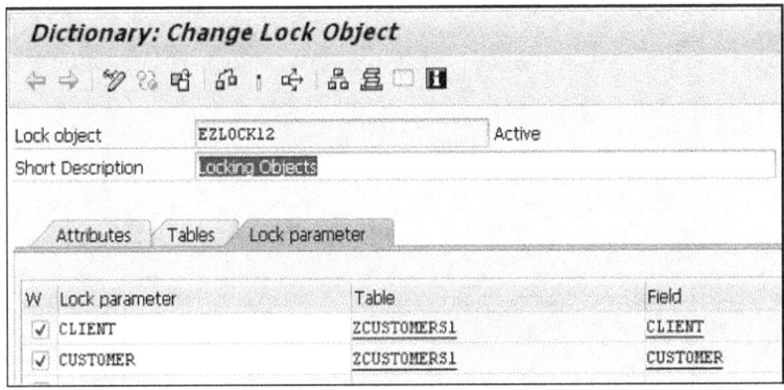



**Step 6** − Save and activate. Automatically 2 function modules will generate. To check function modules, we can use Go to → Lock Modules.

**Step 7** − Click Lock Modules and the following screen will open.

| Repository Info System: Function Modules Find (2 Hits) | |
| --- | --- |
| Function group | Function group short text |
| Function Module Name | Short text for function module |
| /1BCDWBEN/TEN0000 | xRPM 4.0 Demand Planning |
| DEQUEUE_EZLOCK12 | Release lock on object EZLOCK12 |
| ENQUEUE_EZLOCK12 | Request lock for object EZLOCK12 |

The lock object is created successfully.

The key fields of a table included in a Lock Object are called lock arguments and they are used as input parameters in function modules. These arguments are used to set and remove the locks generated by the Lock Object definition.

# SAP ABAP - MODULARIZATION

It is a good practice to keep your programs as self-contained and easy to read as possible. Just try to split large and complicated tasks into smaller and simpler ones by placing each task in its individual module, on which the developer can concentrate on without other distractions.

In SAP ABAP environment, modularization involves the organization of programs into modular units, also known as logical blocks. It reduces redundancy and increases program readability even as you are creating it and subsequently during the maintenance cycle. Modularization also enables reusability of the same code again. ABAP has made it necessary for developers to modularize, i.e. organizing the programs relatively more, than in the OOPS-based languages that have relatively more built-in modular features. Once a small, modularized section of code is complete, debugged and so on, it does not subsequently have to be returned to, and developers can then move on and focus on other issues.

ABAP programs are made up of processing blocks known as modularizing processing blocks. They are —

- ❖ The processing blocks called from outside the program and from the ABAP run-time environment (i.e., event blocks and dialog modules).
- ❖ Processing blocks called from ABAP programs.

Apart from the modularization with processing blocks, source code modules are used to modularize your source code through macros and include programs.

Modularization at source code level —

- ❖ Local Macros
- ❖ Global Include programs

Modularization through processing blocks called from ABAP programs —

- ❖ Subroutines
- ❖ Function modules

Modularizing a source code means placing a sequence of ABAP statements in a module. The modularized source code can be called in a program as per the requirement of the user. Source code modules enhance the readability and understandability of ABAP programs. Creating individual source code modules also prevents one from having to repeatedly write the same statements again and again that in turn makes the code easier to understand for anyone going through it for the first time.

# SAP ABAP - SUBROUTINES

A subroutine is a reusable section of code. It is a modularization unit within the program where a function is encapsulated in the form of source code. You page out a part of a program to a subroutine to get a better overview of the main program, and to use the corresponding sequence of statements many times as depicted in the following diagram.

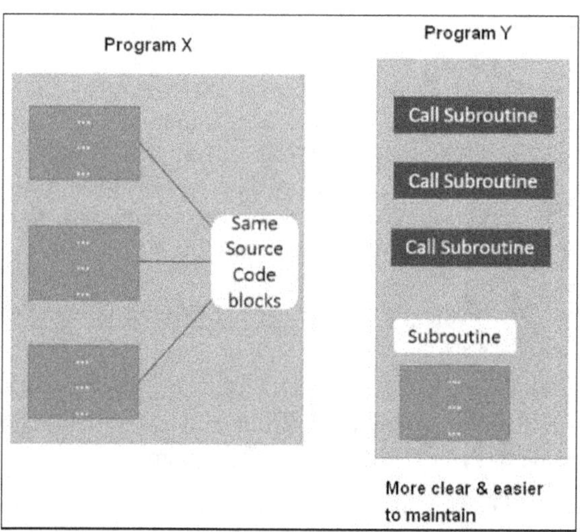


We have program X with 3 different source code blocks. Each block has the same ABAP statements. Basically, they are the same code blocks. To make this code easier to maintain, we can encapsulate the code into a subroutine. We can call this subroutine in our programs as many times as we wish. A subroutine can be defined using Form and EndForm statements.

Following is the general syntax of a subroutine definition.

FORM <subroutine_name>.

<statements>

ENDFORM.

We can call a subroutine by using PERFORM statement. The control jumps to the first executable statement in the subroutine <subroutine_name>. When ENDFORM is encountered, control jumps back to the statement following the PERFORM statement.

# Example

**Step 1** − Go to transaction SE80. Open the existing program and then right-click on program. In this case, it is 'ZSUBTEST'.

**Step 2** − Select Create and then select Subroutine. Write the subroutine name in the field and then click the continue button. The subroutine name is 'Sub_Display' as shown in the following screenshot.

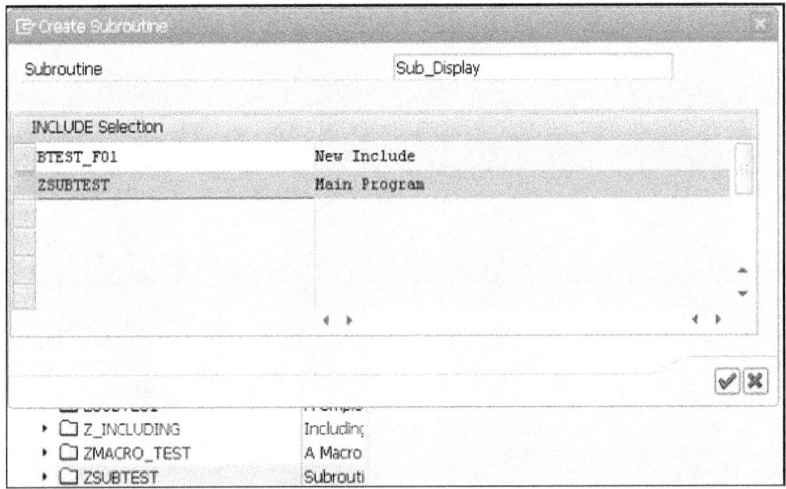



**Step 3** − Write the code in FORM and ENDFORM statement block. The subroutine has been created successfully.

We need to include PERFORM statement to call the subroutine. Let's take a look at the code −

```
REPORT ZSUBTEST.
PERFORM Sub_Display.

* Form Sub_Display
* --> p1 text
* <-- p2 text

FORM Sub_Display.
Write: 'This is Subroutine'.
Write: / 'Subroutine created successfully'.
ENDFORM.                 " Sub_Display
```

**Step 4** − Save, activate and execute the program. The above code produces the following output −

Hence, using subroutines makes your program more function-oriented. It splits the program's task into sub-functions, so that each subroutine is responsible for one subfunction. Your program becomes easier to maintain as changes to functions often only have to be implemented in the subroutine.

If we want to reuse the same set of statements more than once in a program, we need to include them in a macro. For example, a macro can be useful for long calculations or for writing complex WRITE statements. We can only use a macro within a program in which it is defined. Macro definition should occur before the macro is used in the program.

Macros are designed based on placeholders. Placeholder works like pointers in C language. You can define a macro within the DEFINE...END-OF-DEFINITION statement.

Following is the basic syntax of a macro definition −

```
DEFINE <macro_name>. <statements>
END-OF-DEFINITION.

  ......

  <macro_name> [<param1> <param2>....].
```

It is necessary to define a macro first before invoking it. The <param1>.... replaces the placeholders &1...in the ABAP statements contained in the macro definition.

The maximum number of placeholders in a macro definition is nine. That is, when a program is executed, the SAP system replaces the macro by appropriate statements and the placeholders &1, &2,....&9 are replaced by the parameters param1, param2,....param9. We may invoke a macro within another macro, but not the same macro.

## Example

Go to transaction SE38. Create a new program ZMACRO_TEST along with the description in the short text field, and also with appropriate attributes such as Type and Status as shown in the following screenshot −

| Attributes | |
| --- | --- |
| Type | Executable program |
| Status | Test Program |
| Application | |
| Authorization Group | |
| Logical database | |
| Selection screen | |
| ☐ Editor lock | ✓ Fixed point arithmetic |
| ✓ Unicode checks active | ☐ Start using variant |

Following is the code −

```
REPORT ZMACRO_TEST.
DEFINE mac_test.
WRITE: 'This is Macro &1'.
END-OF-DEFINITION.

PARAMETERS: s1 type C as checkbox.
PARAMETERS: s2 type C as checkbox.
PARAMETERS: s3 type C as checkbox default 'X'.

START-OF-SELECTION.
IF s1 = 'X'.
  mac_test 1. ENDIF.
IF s2 = 'X'.
  mac_test 2.
ENDIF.

IF s3 = 'X'.
  mac_test 3.
ENDIF.
```

We have 3 checkboxes. While executing the program, let's select the S2 checkbox.

The above code produces the following output −

A Macro Program

This is Macro 2

If all checkboxes are selected, the code produces the following output —

A Macro Program

This is Macro 1 This is Macro 2 This is Macro 3

# SAP ABAP - FUNCTION MODULES

Function modules make up a major part of a SAP system, because for years SAP has modularized code using function modules, allowing for code reuse, by themselves, their developers and also by their customers.

Function modules are sub-programs that contain a set of reusable statements with importing and exporting parameters. Unlike Include programs, function modules can be executed independently. SAP system contains several predefined function modules that can be called from any ABAP program. The function group acts as a kind of container for a number of function modules that would logically belong together. For instance, the function modules for an HR payroll system would be put together into a function group.

To look at how to create function modules, the function builder must be explored. You can find the function builder with transaction code SE37. Just type a part of a function module name with a wild card character to demonstrate the way function modules can be searched for. Type *amount* and then press the F4 key.

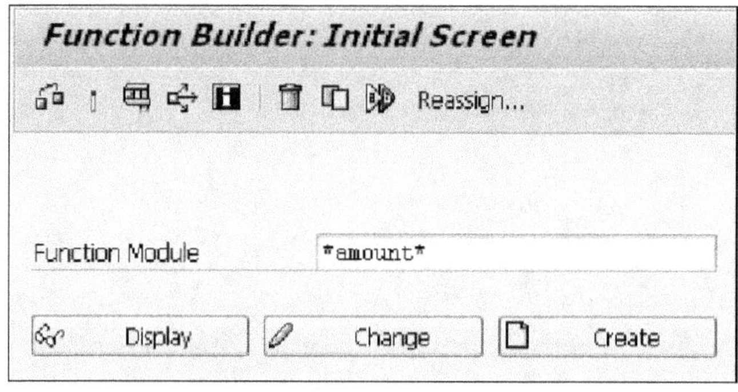


The results of the search will be displayed in a new window. The function modules are displayed in the lines with blue background and their function groups in pink lines. You may look further at the function group ISOC by using the Object Navigator screen (Transaction SE80). You can see a list of function modules and also other objects held in the function group. Let's consider the function module SPELL_AMOUNT. This function module converts numeric figures into words.

## Creating a New Program

**Step 1** − Go to transaction SE38 and create a new program called Z_SPELLAMOUNT.

**Step 2** − Enter some code so that a parameter can be set up where a value could be entered and passed on to the function module. The text element text-001 here reads 'Enter a Value'.

**Step 3** − To write the code for this, use CTRL+F6. After this, a window appears where 'CALL FUNCTION' is the first option in a list. Enter 'spell_amount' in the text box and click the continue button.



**Step 4** − Some code is generated automatically. But we need to enhance the IF statement to include a code to WRITE a message to the screen to say "The function module returned a value of: sy-subrc" and add the ELSE statement so as to write the correct result out when the function module is successful. Here, a new variable must be set up to hold the value returned from the function module. Let's call this as 'result'.

Following is the code −

```
REPORT Z_SPELLAMOUNT.
data result like SPELL.

selection-screen begin of line.
selection-screen comment 1(15) text-001.

parameter num_1 Type I.
selection-screen end of line.
CALL FUNCTION 'SPELL_AMOUNT'
EXPORTING
AMOUNT = num_1
IMPORTING
IN_WORDS = result.

IF SY-SUBRC <> 0.
```

```
   Write: 'Value returned is:', SY-SUBRC.
else.
   Write: 'Amount in words is:', result-word.
ENDIF.
```

**Step 5** − The variable which the function module returns is called IN_WORDS.
Set up the corresponding variable in the program called 'result'. Define
IN_WORDS by using the LIKE statement to refer to a structure called SPELL.

**Step 6** − Save, activate and execute the program. Enter a value as shown in the
following screenshot and press F8.

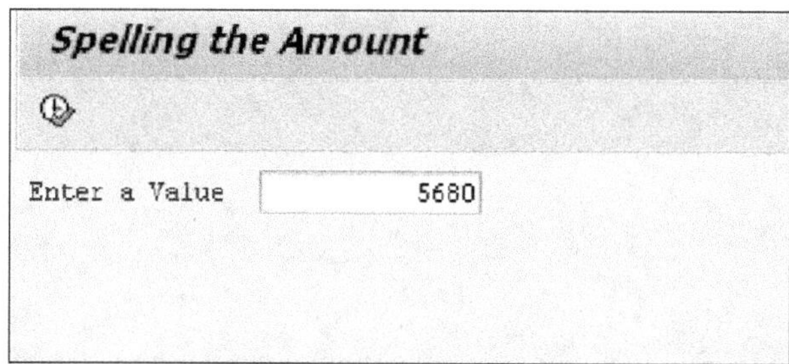


The above code produces the following output −

```
Spelling the Amount
Amount in words is:
FIVE THOUSAND SIX HUNDRED EIGHTY
```

# SAP ABAP - INCLUDE PROGRAMS

Include programs are global repository objects used to modularize the source code.
They allow you to use the same source code in different programs. Include
programs also allow you to manage complex programs in an orderly way. In order
to use an include program in another program, we use the following syntax −

```
INCLUDE <program_name>.
```

INCLUDE statement has the same effect as copying the source code of the include
program <program_name> into another program. As include program can't run
independently, it has to be built into other programs. You may also nest include
programs.

Following are a couple of restrictions while writing the code for Include programs
−

> ❖    Include programs can't call themselves.
> ❖    Include programs must contain complete statements.

Following are the steps to create and use an Include program −

**Step 1** − Create the program (Z_TOBEINCLUDED) to be included in ABAP
Editor. Code to be included in ABAP Editor is −

```
PROGRAM Z_TOBEINCLUDED.
Write: / 'This program is started by:', SY-UNAME,
       / 'The Date is:', SY-DATUM,
       / 'Time is', SY-UZEIT.
```

**Step 2** − Set the Type of the program to INCLUDE program, as shown in the
following screenshot.

Attributes

| Type | INCLUDE program |
| --- | --- |
| Status | Test Program |
| Application | |
| Authorization Group | |

Editor lock

Save

"

**Step 3** − Click the 'Save' button and save the program in a package named ZINCL_PCKG.

**Step 4** − Create another program where the program Z_TOBEINCLUDED has to be used. Here we have created another program named Z_INCLUDINGTEST and assigned the type for the program as Executable program.

**Step 5** − The coding for Z_INCLUDINGTEST program includes the Z_TOBEINCLUDED program with the help of the INCLUDE statement as shown in the following code.

```
REPORT Z_INCLUDINGTEST.
INCLUDE Z_TOBEINCLUDED.
```

**Step 6** − Save, activate and execute the program.

The above code produces the following output −

```
This program is started by: SAPUSER
The Date is: 06.10.2015
Time is 13:25:11
```

# SAP ABAP - OPEN SQL OVERVIEW

Open SQL indicates the subset of ABAP statements that enable direct access to the data in the central database of the current AS ABAP. Open SQL statements map the Data Manipulation Language functionality of SQL in ABAP that is supported by all database systems.

The statements of Open SQL are converted to database specific SQL in the Open SQL interface of the database interface. They are then transferred to the database system and executed. Open SQL statements can be used to access database tables that are declared in the ABAP Dictionary. The central database of AS ABAP is accessed by default and also access to other databases is possible via secondary database connections.

Whenever any of these statements are used in an ABAP program, it is important to check whether the action executed has been successful. If one tries to insert a record into a database table and it is not inserted correctly, it is very essential to know so that the appropriate action can be taken in the program. This can done using a system field that has already been used, that is SY-SUBRC. When a statement is executed successfully, the SY-SUBRC field will contain a value of 0, so this can be checked for and one can continue with the program if it appears.

The DATA statement is used to declare a work area. Let's give this the name 'wa_customers1'. Rather than declaring one data type for this, several fields that make up the table can be declared. The easiest way to do this is using the LIKE statement.

## INSERT Statement

The wa_customers1 work area is declared here LIKE the ZCUSTOMERS1 table, taking on the same structure without becoming a table itself. This work area can only store one record. Once it has been declared, the INSERT statement can be used to insert the work area and the record it holds into the table. The code here will read as 'INSERT ZCUSTOMERS1 FROM wa_customers1'.

The work area has to be filled with some data. Use the field names from the ZCUSTOMERS1 table. This can be done by forward navigation, double clicking the table name in the code or by opening a new session and using the transaction SE11. The fields of the table can then be copied and pasted into the ABAP editor.

Following is the code snippet −

```
DATA wa_customers1 LIKE ZCUSTOMERS1.
```

```
wa_customers1-customer = '100006'.
wa_customers1-name = 'DAVE'.
wa_customers1-title = 'MR'.
wa_customers1-dob = '19931017'.
INSERT ZCUSTOMERS1 FROM wa_customers1.
```

CHECK statement can then be used as follows. It means that if the record is inserted correctly, the system will state this. If not, then the SY-SUBRC code which will not equal zero will be displayed. Following is the code snippet −

```
IF SY-SUBRC = 0.
   WRITE 'Record Inserted Successfully'.
ELSE.
   WRITE: 'The return code is ', SY-SUBRC.
ENDIF.
```

Check the program, save, activate the code, and then test it. The output window should display as 'Record Inserted Successfully'.

## CLEAR Statement

CLEAR statement allows a field or variable to be cleared out for the insertion of new data in its place, allowing it to be reused. CLEAR statement is generally used in programs and it allows existing fields to be used many times.

In the previous code snippet, the work area structure has been filled with data to create a new record to be inserted into the ZCUSTOMERS1 table and then a validation check is performed. If we want to insert a new record, CLEAR statement must be used so that it can then be filled again with the new data.

## UPDATE Statement

If you want to update one or more existing records in a table at the same time then use UPDATE statement. Similar to INSERT statement, a work area is declared, filled with the new data that is then put into the record as the program is executed. The record previously created with the INSERT statement will be updated here. Just edit the text stored in the NAME and TITLE fields. Then on a new line, the same structure as for the INSERT statement is used, and this time by using the UPDATE statement as shown in the following code snippet −

```
DATA wa_customers1 LIKE ZCUSTOMERS1.
wa_customers1-customer = '100006'.
```

```
wa_customers1-name = 'RICHARD'.
wa_customers1-title = 'MR'.
wa_customers1-dob = '19931017'.
UPDATE ZCUSTOMERS1 FROM wa_customers1.
```

As UPDATE statement gets executed, you can view the Data Browser in the ABAP Dictionary to see that the record has been updated successfully.

## MODIFY Statement

MODIFY statement can be considered as a combination of the INSERT and UPDATE statements. It can be used to either insert a new record or modify an existing record. It follows a similar syntax to the previous two statements in modifying the record from the data entered into a work area.

When this statement is executed, the key fields involved will be checked against those in the table. If a record with these key field values already exist, it will be updated. If not, then a new record will be created.

Following is the code snippet for creating a new record −

```
CLEAR wa_customers1.

DATA wa_customers1 LIKE ZCUSTOMERS1.
wa_customers1-customer = '100007'.
wa_customers1-name = 'RALPH'.
wa_customers1-title = 'MR'.
wa_customers1-dob = '19910921'.
MODIFY ZCUSTOMERS1 FROM wa_customers1.
```

In this example, CLEAR statement is used so that a new entry can be put into the work area, and then customer (number) 100007 is added. Since this is a new, unique key field value, a new record will be inserted, and another validation check is executed.

When this is executed and the data is viewed in the Data Browser, a new record will have been created for the customer number 100007 (RALPH).

The above code produces the following output (table contents) −

| Client | Customer Number | Name | Title | DOB |
|---|---|---|---|---|
| 800 | 00100001 | MARK | MR | 21.05.1981 |
| 800 | 00100002 | JAMES | MR | 14.08.1977 |
| 800 | 00100003 | AURIELE | MS | 19.06.1990 |
| 800 | 00100004 | STEPHEN | MR | 22.07.1985 |
| 800 | 00100005 | MARGARET | MS | 02.11.1994 |
| 800 | 00100006 | RICHARD | MR | 17.10.1993 |
| 800 | 00100007 | RALPH | MR | 21.09.1991 |

# SAP ABAP - NATIVE SQL OVERVIEW

The term 'Native SQL' refers to all statements that can be statically transferred to the Native SQL interface of the database interface. Native SQL statements do not fall within the language scope of ABAP and do not follow the ABAP syntax. ABAP merely contains statements for isolating program sections in which Native SQL statements can be listed.

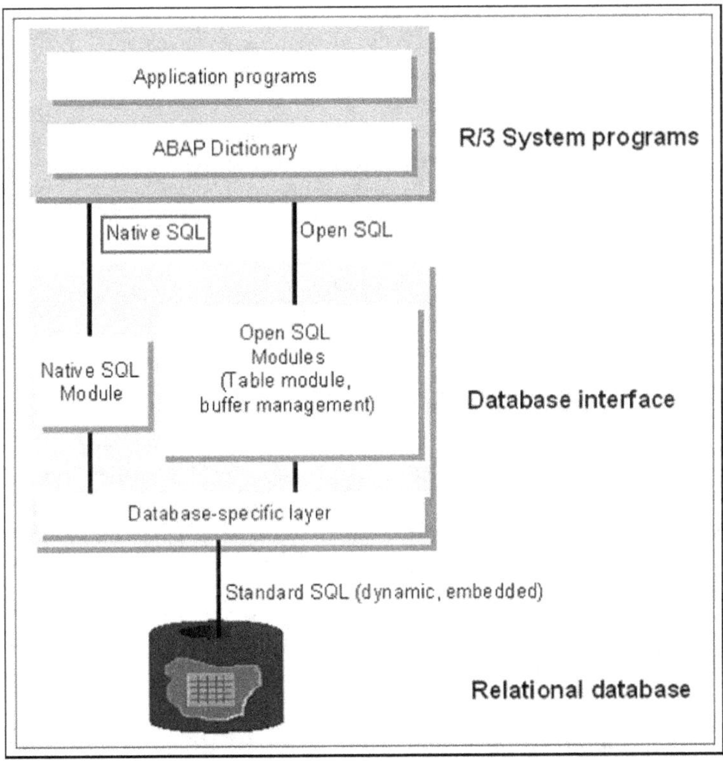


In native SQL, mainly database-specific SQL statements can be used. These are transferred unchanged from the native SQL interface to a database system and executed. The full SQL language scope of the relevant database can be used and the addressed database tables do not have to be declared in the ABAP Dictionary. There is also a small set of SAP specific Native SQL statements that are handled in a specific way by the native SQL interface.

To use a Native SQL statement, you have to precede it with the EXEC SQL statement and end with ENDEXEC statement.

Following is the syntax —

```
EXEC SQL PERFORMING <form>.
  <Native SQL statement>
ENDEXEC.
```

These statements define an area in an ABAP program where one or more Native
SQL statements can be listed. The statements entered are passed to the Native
SQL interface and then processed as follows −

- ❖ All SQL statements that are valid for the program interface of the
  addressed database system can be listed between EXEC and ENDEXEC,
  in particular the DDL (data definition language) statements.
- ❖ These SQL statements are passed from the Native SQL interface to the
  database system largely unchanged. The syntax rules are specified by the
  database system, especially the case sensitivity rules for database objects.
- ❖ If the syntax allows a separator between individual statements, you may
  include many Native SQL statements between EXEC and ENDEXEC.
- ❖ SAP specific Native SQL language elements can be specified between
  EXEC and ENDEXEC. These statements are not passed directly from
  the Native SQL interface to the database, but they are transformed
  appropriately.

## Example

SPFLI is a standard SAP Table that is used to store Flight schedule information.
This is available within R/3 SAP systems depending on the version and release
level. You can view this information when you enter the Table name SPFLI into
the relevant SAP transaction such as SE11 or SE80. You can also view the data
contained in this database table by using these two transactions.

```
REPORT ZDEMONATIVE_SQL.
DATA: BEGIN OF wa,
    connid  TYPE SPFLI-connid,
    cityfrom TYPE SPFLI-cityfrom,
    cityto  TYPE SPFLI-cityto,
    END OF wa.

DATA c1 TYPE SPFLI-carrid VALUE 'LH'.
EXEC SQL PERFORMING loop_output.
  SELECT connid, cityfrom, cityto
  INTO :wa
  FROM SPFLI
  WHERE carrid = :c1
ENDEXEC.

FORM loop_output.
  WRITE: / wa-connid, wa-cityfrom, wa-cityto.
```

ENDFORM.

The above code produces the following output –

```
0400  FRANKFURT  NEW YORK
2402  FRANKFURT  BERLIN
0402  FRANKFURT  NEW YORK
```

# SAP ABAP - INTERNAL TABLES

Internal table is actually a temporary table, which contains the records of an ABAP program that it is being executed. An internal table exists only during the run-time of a SAP program. They are used to process large volumes of data by using ABAP language. We need to declare an internal table in an ABAP program when you need to retrieve data from database tables.

Data in an internal table is stored in rows and columns. Each row is called a line and each column is called a field. In an internal table, all the records have the same structure and key. The individual records of an internal table are accessed with an index or a key. As internal table exists till the associated program is being executed, the records of the internal table are discarded when the execution of the program is terminated. So internal tables can be used as temporary storage areas or temporary buffers where data can be modified as required. These tables occupy memory only at run-time and not at the time of their declaration.

Internal tables only exist when a program is running, so when the code is written, the internal table must be structured in such a way that the program can make use of it. You will find that internal tables operate in the same way as structures. The main difference being that structures only have one line, while an internal table can have as many lines as required.

An internal table can be made up of a number of fields, corresponding to the columns of a table, just as in the ABAP dictionary a table was created using a number of fields. Key fields can also be used with internal tables, and while creating these internal tables they offer slightly more flexibility. With internal tables, one can specify a non-unique key, allowing any number of non-unique records to be stored, and allowing duplicate records to be stored if required.

The size of an internal table or the number of lines it contains is not fixed. The size of an internal table changes according to the requirement of the program associated with the internal table. But it is recommended to keep internal tables as small as possible. This is to avoid the system running slowly as it struggles to process enormous amounts of data.

Internal tables are used for many purposes −

- ❖ They can be used to hold results of calculations that could be used later in the program.
- ❖ An internal table can also hold records and data so that this can be accessed quickly rather than having to access this data from database tables.
- ❖ They are hugely versatile. They can be defined using any number of other defined structures.

## Example

Assume that a user wants to create a list of contact numbers of various customers from one or several large tables. The user first creates an internal table, selects the relevant data from customer tables and then places the data in the internal table. Other users can access and use this internal table directly to retrieve the desired information, instead of writing database queries to perform each operation during the run-time of the program.

# SAP ABAP - CREATING INTERNAL TABLES

DATA statement is used to declare an internal table. The program must be told where the table begins and ends. So use the BEGIN OF statement and then declare the table name. After this, the OCCURS addition is used, followed by a number, here 0. OCCURS tells SAP that an internal table is being created, and the 0 states that it will not contain any records initially. It will then expand as it is filled with data.

Following is the syntax −

DATA: BEGIN OF <internal_tab> Occurs 0,

Let's create the fields on a new line. For instance, create 'name' which is declared as LIKE ZCUSTOMERS1-name. Create another field called 'dob', LIKE ZCUSTOMERS1-dob. It is useful initially to give the field names in internal tables the same names as other fields that have been created elsewhere. Finally, declare the end of the internal table with "END OF <internal_tab>." as shown in the following code −

```
DATA: BEGIN OF itab01 Occurs 0,
   name LIKE ZCUSTOMERS1-name,
   dob LIKE ZCUSTOMERS1-dob,
END OF itab01.
```

Here 'itab01' is commonly used shorthand when creating temporary tables in SAP. The OCCURS clause is used to define the body of an internal table by declaring the fields for the table. When the OCCURS clause is used, you can specify a numeric constant 'n' to determine additional default memory if required. The default size of memory that is used by the OCCUR 0 clause is 8 KB. The structure of the internal table is now created, and the code can be written to fill it with records.

An internal table can be created with or without using a header line. To create an internal table with a header line, use either the BEGIN OF clause before the OCCURS clause or the WITH HEADER LINE clause after the OCCURS clause in the definition of the internal table. To create an internal table without a header line, use the OCCURS clause without the BEGIN OF clause.

You can also create an internal table as a local data type (a data type used only in the context of the current program) by using the TYPES statement. This statement uses the TYPE or LIKE clause to refer to an existing table.

The syntax to create an internal table as a local data type is −

TYPES <internal_tab> TYPE|LIKE <internal_tab_type> OF

<line_type_itab> WITH <key> INITIAL SIZE <size_number>.

---

Here the <internal_tab_type> specifies a table type for an internal table <internal_tab> and <line_type_itab> specifies the type for a line of an internal table. In TYPES statement, you can use the TYPE clause to specify the line type of an internal table as a data type and LIKE clause to specify the line type as a data object. Specifying a key for an internal table is optional and if the user does not specify a key, the SAP system defines a table type with an arbitrary key.

INITIAL SIZE <size_number> creates an internal table object by allocating an initial amount of memory to it. In the preceding syntax, the INITIAL SIZE clause reserves a memory space for size_number table lines. Whenever an internal table object is declared, the size of the table does not belong to the data type of the table.

**Note** − Much less memory is consumed when an internal table is populated for the first time.

# Example

**Step 1** − Open the ABAP Editor by executing the SE38 transaction code. The initial screen of ABAP Editor appears.

**Step 2** − In the initial screen, enter a name for the program, select the Source code radio button and click the Create button to create a new program.

**Step 3** − In the 'ABAP: Program Attributes' dialog box, enter a short description for the program in the Title field, select the 'Executable program' option from the Type drop-down menu in the Attributes group box. Click the Save button.

**Step 4** − Write the following code in ABAP editor.

```
REPORT ZINTERNAL_DEMO.
TYPES: BEGIN OF CustomerLine,
Cust_ID TYPE C,
Cust_Name(20) TYPE C,
END OF CustomerLine.

TYPES mytable TYPE SORTED TABLE OF CustomerLine
WITH UNIQUE KEY Cust_ID.
WRITE:/'The mytable is an Internal Table'.
```

**Step 5** − Save, activate and execute the program as usual.

In this example, mytable is an internal table and a unique key is defined on the Cust_ID field.

The above code produces the following output −

The mytable is an Internal Table.

# SAP ABAP - POPULATING INTERNAL TABLES

In internal tables, populating includes features such as selection, insertion and append. This chapter focuses on INSERT and APPEND statements.

## INSERT Statement

INSERT statement is used to insert a single line or a group of lines into an internal table.

Following is the syntax to add a single line to an internal table −

```
INSERT <work_area_itab> INTO <internal_tab> INDEX <index_num>.
```

In this syntax, the INSERT statement inserts a new line in the internal_tab internal table. A new line can be inserted by using the work_area_itab INTO expression before the internal_tab parameter. When the work_area_itab INTO expression is used, the new line is taken from the work_area_itab work area and inserted into the internal_tab table. However, when the work_area_itab INTO expression is not used to insert a line, the line is taken from the header line of the internal_tab table.

When a new line is inserted in an internal table by using the INDEX clause, the index number of the lines after the inserted line is incremented by 1. If an internal table contains <index_num> - 1 lines, the new line is added at the end of the table. When the SAP system successfully adds a line to an internal table, the SY-SUBRC variable is set to 0.

Example

Following is a sample program that uses the insert statement.

```
REPORT  ZCUSLIST1.
DATA: BEGIN OF itable1 OCCURS 4,
    F1 LIKE SY-INDEX,
    END OF itable1.

  DO 4 TIMES.
    itable1-F1 = sy-index.
    APPEND itable1.
  ENDDO.

itable1-F1 = -96.
INSERT itable1 INDEX 2.
```

```
LOOP AT itable1.
   Write / itable1-F1.
ENDLOOP.

LOOP AT itable1 Where F1 ≥ 3.
   itable1-F1 = -78.
   INSERT itable1.
ENDLOOP.

Skip.
LOOP AT itable1.
   Write / itable1-F1.
ENDLOOP.
```

The above code produces the following outp −

```
                        1
96-
                        2
                        3
4
                        1
96-
                        2
78-
3
78-
4
```

In the above example, the DO loop appends 4 rows containing the numbers 1
through 4 to it. The header line component itable1-F1 has been assigned a value of
-96. Insert statement inserts the header line as new row into the body before row 3.
The existing row 3 becomes row 4 after the insert. The LOOP AT statement
retrieves those rows from the internal table that have an F1 value greater than or
equal to 3. Before each row, Insert statement inserts a new row from the header
line of it. Prior to the insert, the F1 component has been changed to contain -78.

After each insert statement is executed, the system re-indexes all rows below the
one inserted. This introduces overhead when you insert rows near the top of a large
internal table. If you need to insert a block of rows into a large internal table,
prepare another table with the rows to be inserted and use insert lines instead.

When inserting a new row inside itable1 inside of a loop at itable1, it doesn't affect the internal table instantly. It actually becomes effective on the next loop pass. While inserting a row after the current row, the table is re-indexed at the ENDLOOP. The sy-tabix is incremented and the next loop processes the row pointed to by sy-tabix. For instance, if you are in the second loop pass and you insert a record before row 3. When endloop is executed, the new row becomes row 3 and the old row 3 becomes row 4 and so on. Sy-tabix is incremented by 1, and the next loop pass processes the newly inserted record.

## APPEND Statement

The APPEND statement is used to add a single row or line to an existing internal table. This statement copies a single line from a work area and inserts it after the last existing line in an internal table. The work area can be either a header line or any other field string with the same structure as a line of an internal table. Following is the syntax of the APPEND statement that is used to append a single line in an internal table −

```
APPEND <record_for_itab> TO <internal_tab>.
```

In this syntax, the <record_for_itab> expression can be represented by the <work_area_itab> work area, which is convertible to a line type or by the INITIAL LINE clause. If the user uses a <work_area_itab> work area, the SAP system adds a new line to the <internal_tab> internal table and populates it with the content of the work area. The INITIAL LINE clause appends a blank line that contains the initial value for each field of the table structure. After each APPEND statement, the SY-TABIX variable contains the index number of the appended line.

Appending lines to standard and sorted tables with a non-unique key works regardless of whether the lines with the same key already exist in the table. In other words, duplicate entries may occur. However, a run-time error occurs if the user attempts to add a duplicate entry to a sorted table with a unique key or if the user violates the sort order of a sorted table by appending the lines to it.

## Example

```
REPORT ZCUSLIST1.
DATA: BEGIN OF linv Occurs 0,
     Name(20) TYPE C,
     ID_Number TYPE I,
END OF linv.

DATA table1 LIKE TABLE OF linv.
```

```
linv-Name = 'Melissa'.
linv-ID_Number = 105467.
APPEND linv TO table1.
LOOP AT table1 INTO linv.

Write: / linv-name, linv-ID_Number.
ENDLOOP.
```

The above code produces the following output –

```
Melissa            105467
```

When we read a record from an internal table with a header line, that record is moved from the table itself into the header line. It is then the header line that our program works with. The same applies while creating a new record. It is the header line with which you work with and from which the new record is sent to the table body itself.

To copy the records, we can use a SELECT statement to select all of the records from the table and then use MOVE statement that will move the records from the original table into the new internal table into the fields where the names correspond.

Following is the syntax for MOVE statement −

```
MOVE <table_field> TO <internal_tab_field>.
```

# Example

```
REPORT  ZCUSLIST1.
TABLES: ZCUSTOMERS1.
DATA: BEGIN OF itab01 Occurs 0,
    name LIKE ZCUSTOMERS1-name,
    dob LIKE ZCUSTOMERS1-dob,
END OF itab01.

Select * FROM ZCUSTOMERS1.
MOVE ZCUSTOMERS1-name TO itab01-name.
MOVE ZCUSTOMERS1-dob TO itab01-dob.
ENDSELECT.

Write: / itab01-name, itab01-dob.
```

The above code produces the following output −

```
MARGARET            02.11.1994
```

The select loop fills each field one at a time, using the MOVE statement to move the data from one table's field to the other. In the above example, MOVE statements were used to move the contents of the ZCUSTOMERS1 table to the corresponding fields in the internal table. You can accomplish this action with just one line of code. You can use the MOVECORRESPONDING statement.

Following is the syntax for MOVE-CORRESPONDING statement −

MOVE-CORRESPONDING <table_name> TO <internal_tab>.

It tells the system to move the data from the fields of ZCUSTOMERS1 to their corresponding fields in itab01.

## Example

```
REPORT  ZCUSTOMERLIST.
TABLES: ZCUSTOMERS1.
DATA: Begin of itab01 occurs 0,
     customer LIKE ZCUSTOMERS1-customer,
     name LIKE ZCUSTOMERS1-name,
     title LIKE ZCUSTOMERS1-title,
     dob LIKE ZCUSTOMERS1-dob,
END OF itab01.

SELECT * from ZCUSTOMERS1.
MOVE-Corresponding ZCUSTOMERS1 TO itab01.
APPEND itab01.
ENDSELECT.
LOOP AT itab01.
Write: / itab01-name, itab01-dob.
ENDLOOP.
```

The above code produces the following output −

```
MARK        21.05.1981
JAMES       14.08.1977
AURIELE     19.06.1990
STEPHEN     22.07.1985
MARGARET    02.11.1994
```

This is made possible by the fact that both have matching field names. When making use of this statement, you need to make sure that both fields have matching data types and lengths. It has been done here with the LIKE statement previously.

# SAP ABAP - READING INTERNAL TABLES

We can read the lines of a table by using the following syntax of the READ TABLE statement −

```
READ TABLE <internal_table> FROM <work_area_itab>.
```

In this syntax, the <work_area_itab> expression represents a work area that is compatible with the line type of the <internal_table> table. We can specify a search key, but not a table key, within the READ statement by using the WITH KEY clause, as shown in the following syntax −

```
READ TABLE <internal_table> WITH KEY = <internal_tab_field>.
```

Here the entire line of the internal table is used as a search key. The content of the entire line of the table is compared with the content of the <internal_tab_field> field. If the values of the <internal_tab_field> field are not compatible with the line type of the table, these values are converted according to the line type of the table. The search key allows you to find entries in internal tables that do not have a structured line type, that is, where the line is a single field or an internal table type.

The following syntax of the READ statement is used to specify a work area or field symbol by using the COMPARING clause −

```
READ TABLE <internal_table> <key> INTO <work_area_itab>
  [COMPARING <F1> <F2>...<Fn>].
```

When the COMPARING clause is used, the specified table fields <F1>, <F2>....<Fn> of the structured line type are compared with the corresponding fields of the work area before being transported. If the ALL FIELDS clause is specified, the SAP system compares all the components. When the SAP system finds an entry on the basis of a key, the value of the SY-SUBRC variable is set to 0. In addition, the value of the SY-SUBRC variable is set to 2 or 4 if the content of the compared fields is not the same or if the SAP system cannot find an entry. However, the SAP system copies the entry into the target work area whenever it finds an entry, regardless of the result of the comparison.

## Example

```
REPORT ZREAD_DEMO.
*/Creating an internal table
DATA: BEGIN OF Record1,
ColP TYPE I,
```

```
ColQ TYPE I,
END OF Record1.

DATA mytable LIKE HASHED TABLE OF Record1 WITH UNIQUE KEY
ColP.
DO 6 Times.
Record1-ColP = SY-INDEX.
Record1-ColQ = SY-INDEX + 5.
INSERT Record1 INTO TABLE mytable.
ENDDO.

Record1-ColP = 4.
Record1-ColQ = 12.
READ TABLE mytable FROM Record1 INTO Record1 COMPARING ColQ.

WRITE: 'SY-SUBRC =', SY-SUBRC.
SKIP.
WRITE: / Record1-ColP, Record1-ColQ.
```

The above code produces the following output −

```
SY-SUBRC =   2


4     9
```

In the above example, mytable is an internal table of the hashed table type, with Record1 as the work area and ColP as the unique key. Initially, mytable is populated with six lines, where the ColP field contains the values of the SY-INDEX variable and the ColQ field contains (SY-INDEX + 5) values.

The Record1 work area is populated with 4 and 12 as values for the ColP and ColQ fields respectively. The READ statement reads the line of the table after comparing the value of the ColP key field with the value in the Record1 work area by using the COMPARING clause, and then copies the content of the read line in the work area. The value of the SY-SUBRC variable is displayed as 2 because when the value in the ColP field is 4, the value in the ColQ is not 12, but 9.

# SAP ABAP - DELETING INTERNAL TABLES

The DELETE statement is used to delete one or more records from an internal table. The records of an internal table are deleted either by specifying a table key or condition or by finding duplicate entries. If an internal table has a non-unique key and contains duplicate entries, the first entry from the table is deleted.

Following is the syntax to use the DELETE statement to delete a record or line from an internal table −

DELETE TABLE <internal_table> FROM <work_area_itab>.

In the above syntax, the <work_area_itab> expression is a work area and it should be compatible with the type of the <internal_table> internal table. The delete operation is performed on the basis of a default key that could be taken from the work area components.

You may also specify a table key explicitly in the DELETE TABLE statement by using the following syntax −

DELETE TABLE <internal_table> WITH TABLE KEY <K1> =
<F1>............ <Kn> = <Fn>.

In this syntax, <F1>, <F2>....<Fn> are the fields of an internal table and <K1>, <K2>....<Kn> are the key fields of the table. The DELETE statement is used to delete the records or lines of the <internal_table> table based on the expressions <K1> = <F1>, <K2> = <F2>...<Kn> = <Fn>.

**Note** − If the data types of the <F1>, <F2>....<Fn> fields are not compatible with the <K1>, <K2>...<Kn> key fields then the SAP system automatically converts them into the compatible format.


# Example

```
REPORT  ZDELETE_DEMO.
DATA: BEGIN OF Line1,
ColP TYPE I,
ColQ TYPE I,
END OF Line1.
DATA mytable LIKE HASHED TABLE OF Line1
WITH UNIQUE KEY ColP.
DO 8 TIMES.
```

```
Line1-ColP = SY-INDEX.
Line1-ColQ = SY-INDEX + 4.
INSERT Line1 INTO TABLE mytable.
ENDDO.

Line1-ColP = 1.
DELETE TABLE mytable: FROM Line1,
WITH TABLE KEY ColP = 3.
LOOP AT mytable INTO Line1.

WRITE: / Line1-ColP, Line1-ColQ.
ENDLOOP.
```

The above code produces the following output –

| | |
|---|---|
| 2 | 6 |
| 4 | 8 |
| 5 | 9 |
| 6 | 10 |
| 7 | 11 |
| 8 | 12 |

In this example, mytable has two fields, ColP and ColQ. Initially, mytable is populated with eight lines, where the ColP contains the values 1, 2, 3, 4, 5, 6, 7 and 8. The ColQ contains the values 5, 6, 7, 8, 9, 10, 11 and 12 because the ColP values are incremented by 4 every time.

The DELETE statement is used to delete the lines from mytable where the value of the ColP key field is either 1 or 3. After deletion, the ColP field of mytable contains the values 2, 4, 5, 6, 7 and 8, as shown in the output. The ColQ field contains the values 6, 8, 9, 10, 11 and 12.

# SAP ABAP - OBJECT ORIENTATION

Object orientation simplifies software design to make it easier to understand, maintain, and reuse. Object Oriented Programming (OOP) represents a different way of thinking in writing software. The beauty of OOP lies in its simplicity. The expressiveness of OOP makes it easier to deliver quality software components on time.

As solutions are designed in terms of real-world objects, it becomes much easier for programmers and business analysts to exchange ideas and information about a design that uses a common domain language. These improvements in communication help to reveal hidden requirements, identify risks, and improve the quality of software being developed. The object-oriented approach focuses on objects that represent abstract or concrete things of the real world. These objects are defined by their character and properties that are represented by their internal structure and their attributes (data). The behavior of these objects is described by methods (i.e. functionality).

Let's compare the procedural and object oriented programming −

| Features | Procedure Oriented approach | Object Oriented approach |
| --- | --- | --- |
| Emphasis | Emphasis is on tasks. | Emphasis is on things that does those tasks. |
| Modularization | Programs can be divided into smaller programs known as functions. | Programs are organized into classes and objects and the functionalities are embedded into methods of a class. |
| Data security | Most of the functions share global data. | Data can be hidden and can't be accessed by external sources. |
| Extensibility | This is more time consuming to modify and extend the existing functionality. | New data and functions can be added effortlessly as and when required. |

ABAP was initially developed as a procedural language (just similar to earlier procedural programming language like COBOL). But ABAP has now adapted the principles of object oriented paradigms with the introduction of ABAP Objects. The object-oriented concepts in ABAP such as class, object, inheritance, and polymorphism, are essentially the same as those of other modern object-oriented languages such as Java or C++.

As object orientation begins to take shape, each class assumes specific role assignments. This division of labor helps to simplify the overall programming model, allowing each class to specialize in solving a particular piece of the problem at hand. Such classes have high cohesion and the operations of each class are closely related in some intuitive way.

The key features of object orientation are –

- ❖ Effective programming structure.
- ❖ Real-world entities can be modeled very well.
- ❖ Stress on data security and access.
- ❖ Minimizes code redundancy.
- ❖ Data abstraction and encapsulation.

# AP ABAP - OBJECTS

An object is a special kind of variable that has distinct characteristics and behaviors. The characteristics or attributes of an object are used to describe the state of an object, and behaviors or methods represent the actions performed by an object.

An object is a pattern or instance of a class. It represents a real-world entity such as a person or a programming entity like variables and constants. For example, accounts and students are examples of real-world entities. But hardware and software components of a computer are examples of programming entities.

An object has the following three main characteristics −

- ❖ Has a state.
- ❖ Has a unique identity.
- ❖ May or may not display the behavior.

The state of an object can be described as a set of attributes and their values. For example, a bank account has a set of attributes such as Account Number, Name, Account Type, Balance, and values of all these attributes. The behavior of an object refers to the changes that occur in its attributes over a period of time.

Each object has a unique identity that can be used to distinguish it from other objects. Two objects may exhibit the same behavior and they may or may not have the same state, but they never have the same identity. Two persons may have the same name, age, and gender but they are not identical. Similarly, the identity of an object will never change throughout its lifetime.

Objects can interact with one another by sending messages. Objects contain data and code to manipulate the data. An object can also be used as a user-defined data type with the help of a class. Objects are also called variables of the type class. After defining a class, you can create any number of objects belonging to that class. Each object is associated with the data of the type class with which it has been created.

## Creating an Object

The object creation usually includes the following steps −

- ❖ Creating a reference variable with reference to the class. The syntax for which is −

```
DATA: <object_name> TYPE REF TO <class_name>.
```

- ❖ Creating an object from the reference variable. The syntax for which is −

```
CREATE Object: <object_name>.
```

## Example

```
REPORT ZDEMO_OBJECT.
CLASS Class1 Definition.
Public Section.
DATA: text1(45) VALUE 'ABAP Objects.'.
METHODS: Display1.
ENDCLASS.

CLASS Class1 Implementation.
METHOD Display1.
Write:/ 'This is the Display method.'.
ENDMETHOD.
ENDCLASS.

START-OF-SELECTION.
DATA: Class1 TYPE REF TO Class1.
CREATE Object: Class1.
Write:/ Class1->text1.
CALL METHOD: Class1->Display1.
```

The above code produces the following output −

```
ABAP Objects.
This is the Display method.
```

# SAP ABAP - CLASSES

A class is used to specify the form of an object and it combines data representation and methods for manipulating that data into one neat package. The data and functions within a class are called members of the class.

## Class Definition and Implementation

When you define a class, you define a blueprint for a data type. This doesn't actually define any data, but it does define what the class name means, what an object of the class will consist of, and what operations can be performed on such an object. That is, it defines the abstract characteristics of an object, such as attributes, fields, and properties.

The following syntax shows how to define a class −

```
CLASS <class_name> DEFINITION.
..........
..........
ENDCLASS.
```

A class definition starts with the keyword CLASS followed by the class name, DEFINITION and the class body. The definition of a class can contain various components of the class such as attributes, methods, and events. When we declare a method in the class declaration, the method implementation must be included in the class implementation. The following syntax shows how to implement a class −

```
CLASS <class_name> IMPLEMENTATION.
...........
..........
ENDCLASS.
```

**Note** − Implementation of a class contains the implementation of all its methods. In ABAP Objects, the structure of a class contains components such as attributes, methods, events, types, and constants.

## Attributes

Attributes are data fields of a class that can have any data type such as C, I, F, and N. They are declared in the class declaration. These attributes can be divided into 2 categories: instance and static attributes. An instance attribute defines the instance specific state of an object. The states are different for different objects. An instance attribute is declared by using the DATA statement.

Static attributes define a common state of a class that is shared by all the instances of the class. That is, if you change a static attribute in one object of a class, the change is visible to all other objects of the class as well. A static attribute is declared by using the CLASS-DATA statement.

## Methods

A method is a function or procedure that represents the behavior of an object in the class. The methods of the class can access any attribute of the class. The definition of a method can also contain parameters, so that you can supply the values to these parameters when methods are called. The definition of a method is declared in the class declaration and implemented in the implementation part of a class. The METHOD and ENDMETHOD statements are used to define the implementation part of a method. The following syntax shows how to implement a method −

```
METHOD <m_name>.
..........
..........
ENDMETHOD.
```

In this syntax, <m_name> represents the name of a method. Note − You can call a method by using the CALL METHOD statement.

## Accessing Attributes and Methods

Class components can be defined in public, private, or protected visibility sections that control how these components could be accessed. The private visibility section is used to deny access to components from outside of the class. Such components can only be accessed from inside the class such as a method.

Components defined in the public visibility section can be accessed from any context. By default all the members of a class would be private. Practically, we define data in private section and related methods in public section so that they can be called from outside of the class as shown in the following program.

- ❖ The attributes and methods declared in Public section in a class can be accessed by that class and any other class, sub-class of the program.
- ❖ When the attributes and methods are declared in Protected section in a class, those can be accessed by that class and sub classes (derived classes) only.
- ❖ When the attributes and methods are declared in Private section in a class, those can be accessed by only that class and not by any other class.
- ❖ Example

```
Report ZAccess1.
CLASS class1 Definition.
  PUBLIC Section.
    Data: text1 Type char25 Value 'Public Data'.
    Methods meth1.

  PROTECTED Section.
    Data: text2 Type char25 Value 'Protected Data'.

  PRIVATE Section.
    Data: text3 Type char25 Value 'Private Data'.
ENDCLASS.

CLASS class1 Implementation.
  Method meth1.
    Write: / 'Public Method:',
        / text1,
        / text2,
        / text3.
    Skip.
  EndMethod.
ENDCLASS.

Start-Of-Selection.
  Data: Objectx Type Ref To class1.
  Create Object: Objectx.
  CALL Method: Objectx→meth1.
  Write: / Objectx→text1.
```

The above code produces the following output −

```
Public Method:
Public Data
```

Protected Data
Private Data

Public Data

## Static Attributes

A Static attribute is declared with the statement CLASS-DATA. All the objects or instances can use the static attribute of the class. Static attributes are accessed directly with the help of class name like class_name⇒name_1 = 'Some Text'.

## Example

Following is a program where we want to print a text with line number 4 to 8 times. We define a class class1 and in the public section we declare CLASS-DATA (static attribute) and a method. After implementing the class and method, we directly access the static attribute in Start-Of-Selection event. Then we just create the instance of the class and call the method.

```
Report ZStatic1.
CLASS class1 Definition.
  PUBLIC Section.
    CLASS-DATA: name1 Type char45,
            data1 Type I.
  Methods: meth1.
ENDCLASS.

CLASS class1 Implementation.
  Method meth1.
    Do 4 Times.
      data1 = 1 + data1.
      Write: / data1, name1.
    EndDo.
    Skip.
  EndMethod.
ENDCLASS.

Start-Of-Selection.
  class1⇒name1 = 'ABAP Object Oriented Programming'.
  class1⇒data1 = 0.
  Data: Object1 Type Ref To class1,
      Object2 Type Ref To class1.
```

```
Create Object: Object1, Object2.
CALL Method: Object1→meth1,
             Object2→meth1.
```

The above code produces the following output −

| Static Attributes |
| --- |
| |
| Static Attributes |
| 1  ABAP Object Oriented Programming |
| 2  ABAP Object Oriented Programming |
| 3  ABAP Object Oriented Programming |
| 4  ABAP Object Oriented Programming |
| |
| 5  ABAP Object Oriented Programming |
| 6  ABAP Object Oriented Programming |
| 7  ABAP Object Oriented Programming |
| 8  ABAP Object Oriented Programming |

## Constructors

Constructors are special methods that are called automatically, either while creating an object or accessing the components of a class. Constructor gets triggered whenever an object is created, but we need to call a method to trigger the general method. In the following example, we have declared two public methods method1 and constructor. Both these methods have different operations. While creating an object of the class, the constructor method triggers its operation.

## Example

```
Report ZConstructor1.
CLASS class1 Definition.
  PUBLIC Section.
    Methods: method1, constructor.
ENDCLASS.

CLASS class1 Implementation.
  Method method1.
    Write: / 'This is Method1'.
  EndMethod.
```

```
Method constructor.
  Write: / 'Constructor Triggered'.
EndMethod.
ENDCLASS.

Start-Of-Selection.
  Data Object1 Type Ref To class1.
  Create Object Object1.
```

The above code produces the following output −

```
Constructor Triggered
```

## ME Operator in Methods

When you declare a variable of any type in public section of a class, you can use it
in any other implementation. A variable can be declared with an initial value in
public section. We may declare the variable again inside a method with a different
value. When we write the variable inside the method, the system will print the
changed value. To reflect the previous value of the variable, we have to use 'ME'
operator.

In this program, we have declared a public variable text1 and initiated with a value.
We have declared the same variable again, but instantiated with different value.
Inside the method, we are writing that variable with 'ME' operator to get the
previously initiated value. We get the changed value by declaring directly.

## Example

```
Report ZMEOperator1.
CLASS class1 Definition.
  PUBLIC Section.

Data text1 Type char25 Value 'This is CLASS Attribute'.
  Methods method1.
ENDCLASS.

CLASS class1 Implementation.
  Method method1.

Data text1 Type char25 Value 'This is METHOD Attribute'.
```

```
  Write: / ME→text1,
      / text1.
  ENDMethod.
ENDCLASS.

Start-Of-Selection.
  Data objectx Type Ref To class1.
  Create Object objectx.
  CALL Method objectx→method1.
```

The above code produces the following output −

```
This is CLASS Attribute
This is METHOD Attribute
```

# SAP ABAP - INHERITANCE

One of the most important concepts in object oriented programming is that of inheritance. Inheritance allows us to define a class in terms of another class, which makes it easier to create and maintain an application. This also provides an opportunity to reuse the code functionality and fast implementation time.

When creating a class, instead of writing completely new data members and methods, the programmer can designate that the new class should inherit the members of an existing class. This existing class is called the base class or super class, and the new class is referred to as the derived class or sub class.

- ❖ An object of one class can acquire the properties of another class.
- ❖ Derived class inherits the data and methods of a super class. However, they can overwrite methods and also add new methods.
- ❖ The main advantage of inheritance is reusability.

The inheritance relationship is specified using the 'INHERITING FROM' addition to the class definition statement.

Following is the syntax −

```
CLASS <subclass> DEFINITION INHERITING FROM <superclass>.
```

## Example

```
Report ZINHERITAN_1.
CLASS Parent Definition.
PUBLIC Section.
Data: w_public(25) Value 'This is public data'.
Methods: ParentM.
ENDCLASS.

CLASS Child Definition Inheriting From Parent.
PUBLIC Section.
Methods: ChildM.
ENDCLASS.

CLASS Parent Implementation.
Method ParentM.
Write /: w_public.
EndMethod. ENDCLASS.

CLASS Child Implementation.
```

```
Method ChildM.
Skip.
Write /: 'Method in child class', w_public.
EndMethod.
ENDCLASS.

Start-of-selection.
Data: Parent Type Ref To Parent,
Child Type Ref To Child.
Create Object: Parent, Child.
Call Method: Parent→ParentM,
child→ChildM.
```

The above code produces the following output −

```
This is public data
Method in child class
This is public data
```

## Access Control and Inheritance

A derived class can access all the non-private members of its base class. Thus super class members that should not be accessible to the member functions of sub classes should be declared private in the super class. We can summarize the different access types according to who can access them in the following way −

| Access | Public | Protected | Private |
|---|---|---|---|
| Same calss | Yes | Yes | Yes |
| Derived class | Yes | Yes | No |
| Outside class | Yes | No | No |

When deriving a class from a super class, it can be inherited through public, protected or private inheritance. The type of inheritance is specified by the access specifier as explained above. We hardly use protected or private inheritance, but public inheritance is commonly used. The following rules are applied while using different types of inheritance.

- ❖ **Public Inheritance** − When deriving a class from a public super class, public members of the super class become public members of the sub class and protected members of the super class become protected members of the sub class. Super class's private members are never accessible directly from a sub class, but can be accessed through calls to the public and protected members of the super class.

- ❖ **Protected Inheritance** – When deriving from a protected super class, public and protected members of the super class become protected members of the sub class.
- ❖ **Private Inheritance** – When deriving from a private super class, public and protected members of the super class become private members of the sub class.

## Redefining Methods in Sub Class

The methods of the super class can be re-implemented in the sub class. Few rules of redefining methods –

- ❖ The redefinition statement for the inherited method must be in the same section as the definition of the original method.
- ❖ If you redefine a method, you do not need to enter its interface again in the subclass, but only the name of the method.
- ❖ Within the redefined method, you can access components of the direct super class using the super reference.
- ❖ The pseudo reference super can only be used in redefined methods.

## Example

```
Report Zinheri_Redefine.
CLASS super_class Definition.
Public Section.
Methods: Addition1 importing g_a TYPE I
                    g_b TYPE I
                        exporting g_c TYPE I.
ENDCLASS.

CLASS super_class Implementation.
Method Addition1.
g_c = g_a + g_b.
EndMethod.
ENDCLASS.

CLASS sub_class Definition Inheriting From super_class.
Public Section.
METHODS: Addition1 Redefinition.
ENDCLASS.

CLASS sub_class Implementation.
Method Addition1.
```

g_c = g_a + g_b + 10.
EndMethod.
ENDCLASS.

Start-Of-Selection.
Parameters: P_a Type I, P_b TYPE I.
Data: H_Addition1 TYPE I.
Data: H_Sub TYPE I.
Data: Ref1 TYPE Ref TO sub_class.
Create Object Ref1.
Call Method Ref1→Addition1 exporting g_a = P_a
                      g_b = P_b
                           Importing g_c = H_Addition1.
Write:/ H_Addition1.

After executing F8, if we enter the values 9 and 10, the above code produces the following output −

P_A                                        9
P_B                                       10

Redefinition Demo
29

# SAP ABAP - POLYMORPHISM

The term polymorphism literally means 'many forms'. From an object-oriented perspective, polymorphism works in conjunction with inheritance to make it possible for various types within an inheritance tree to be used interchangeably. That is, polymorphism occurs when there is a hierarchy of classes and they are related by inheritance. ABAP polymorphism means that a call to a method will cause a different method to be executed depending on the type of object that invokes the method.

The following program contains an abstract class 'class_prgm', 2 sub classes (class_procedural and class_OO), and a test driver class 'class_type_approach'. In this implementation, the class method 'start' allow us to display the type of programming and its approach. If you look closely at the signature of method 'start', you will observe that it receives an importing parameter of type class_prgm. However, in the Start-Of-Selection event, this method has been called at run-time with objects of type class_procedural and class_OO.

## Example

```
Report ZPolymorphism1.
CLASS class_prgm Definition Abstract.
PUBLIC Section.
Methods: prgm_type Abstract,
approach1 Abstract.
ENDCLASS.

CLASS class_procedural Definition
Inheriting From class_prgm.
PUBLIC Section.
Methods: prgm_type Redefinition,
approach1 Redefinition.
ENDCLASS.

CLASS class_procedural Implementation.
Method prgm_type.
Write: 'Procedural programming'.

EndMethod. Method approach1.
Write: 'top-down approach'.

EndMethod. ENDCLASS.
CLASS class_OO Definition
Inheriting From class_prgm.
```

```
PUBLIC Section.
Methods: prgm_type Redefinition,
approach1 Redefinition.
ENDCLASS.

CLASS class_OO Implementation.
Method prgm_type.
Write: 'Object oriented programming'.
EndMethod.

Method approach1.
Write: 'bottom-up approach'.
EndMethod.
ENDCLASS.

CLASS class_type_approach Definition.
PUBLIC Section.
CLASS-METHODS:
start Importing class1_prgm
Type Ref To class_prgm.
ENDCLASS.

CLASS class_type_approach IMPLEMENTATION.
Method start.
CALL Method class1_prgm→prgm_type.
Write: 'follows'.

CALL Method class1_prgm→approach1.
EndMethod.
ENDCLASS.

Start-Of-Selection.
Data: class_1 Type Ref To class_procedural,
class_2 Type Ref To class_OO.

Create Object class_1.
Create Object class_2.
CALL Method class_type_approach⇒start
Exporting

class1_prgm = class_1.
New-Line.
CALL Method class_type_approach⇒start
Exporting
class1_prgm = class_2.
```

The above code produces the following output −

ABAP run-time environment performs an implicit narrowing cast during the assignment of the importing parameter class1_prgm. This feature helps the 'start' method to be implemented generically. The dynamic type information associated with an object reference variable allows the ABAP run-time environment to dynamically bind a method call with the implementation defined in the object pointed to by the object reference variable. For instance, the importing parameter 'class1_prgm' for method 'start' in the 'class_type_approach' class refers to an abstract type that could never be instantiated on its own.

Whenever the method is called with a concrete sub class implementation such as class_procedural or class_OO, the dynamic type of the class1_prgm reference parameter is bound to one of these concrete types. Therefore, the calls to methods 'prgm_type' and 'approach1' refer to the implementations provided in the class_procedural or class_OO sub classes rather than the undefined abstract implementations provided in class 'class_prgm'.

# SAP ABAP - ENCAPSULATION

Encapsulation is an Object Oriented Programming (OOP) concept that binds together data and functions that manipulate the data, and keeps both safe from outside interference and misuse. Data encapsulation led to the important OOP concept of data hiding. Encapsulation is a mechanism of bundling the data and the functions that use them, and data abstraction is a mechanism of exposing only the interfaces and hiding the implementation details from the user.

ABAP supports the properties of encapsulation and data hiding through the creation of user-defined types called classes. As discussed earlier, a class can contain private, protected and public members. By default, all items defined in a class are private.

## Encapsulation by Interface

Encapsulation actually means one attribute and method could be modified in different classes. Hence data and method can have different form and logic that can be hidden to separate class.

Let's consider encapsulation by interface. Interface is used when we need to create one method with different functionality in different classes. Here the name of the method need not be changed. The same method will have to be implemented in different class implementations.

## Example

The following program contains an Interface inter_1. We have declared attribute and a method method1. We have also defined two classes like Class1 and Class2. So we have to implement the method 'method1' in both of the class implementations. We have implemented the method 'method1' differently in different classes. In the start-ofselection, we create two objects Object1 and Object2 for two classes. Then, we call the method by different objects to get the function declared in separate classes.

```
Report ZEncap1.
Interface inter_1.
   Data text1 Type char35.
   Methods method1.
EndInterface.

CLASS Class1 Definition.
```

```abap
  PUBLIC Section.
    Interfaces inter_1.
ENDCLASS.

CLASS Class2 Definition.
  PUBLIC Section.
    Interfaces inter_1.
ENDCLASS.

CLASS Class1 Implementation.
  Method inter_1~method1.
    inter_1~text1 = 'Class 1 Interface method'.
    Write / inter_1~text1.
  EndMethod.
ENDCLASS.

CLASS Class2 Implementation.
  Method inter_1~method1.
    inter_1~text1 = 'Class 2 Interface method'.
    Write / inter_1~text1.
  EndMethod.
ENDCLASS.

Start-Of-Selection.
  Data: Object1 Type Ref To Class1,
    Object2 Type Ref To Class2.

  Create Object: Object1, Object2.
  CALL Method: Object1→inter_1~method1,
          Object2→inter_1~method1.
```

The above code produces the following output −

```
Class 1 Interface method
Class 2 Interface method
```

Encapsulated classes do not have a lot of dependencies on the outside world. Moreover, the interactions that they do have with external clients are controlled through a stabilized public interface. That is, an encapsulated class and its clients are loosely coupled. For the most part, classes with well-defined interfaces can be plugged into another context. When designed correctly, encapsulated classes become reusable software assets.

# Designing Strategy

Most of us have learned through bitter experience to make class members private by default unless we really need to expose them. That is just good encapsulation. This wisdom is applied most frequently to data members and it also applies equally to all members.

# SAP ABAP - INTERFACES

Similar to classes in ABAP, interfaces act as data types for objects. The components of interfaces are same as the components of classes. Unlike the declaration of classes, the declaration of an interface does not include the visibility sections. This is because the components defined in the declaration of an interface are always integrated in the public visibility section of the classes.

Interfaces are used when two similar classes have a method with the same name, but the functionalities are different from each other. Interfaces might appear similar to classes, but the functions defined in an interface are implemented in a class to extend the scope of that class. Interfaces along with the inheritance feature provide a base for polymorphism. This is because a method defined in an interface can behave differently in different classes.

Following is the general format to create an interface −

```
INTERFACE <intf_name>.
DATA.....
CLASS-DATA.....
METHODS.....
CLASS-METHODS.....
ENDINTERFACE.
```

In this syntax, <intf_name> represents the name of an interface. The DATA and CLASSDATA statements can be used to define the instance and static attributes of the interface respectively. The METHODS and CLASS-METHODS statements can be used to define the instance and static methods of the interface respectively. As the definition of an interface does not include the implementation class, it is not necessary to add the DEFINITION clause in the declaration of an interface.

**Note** − All the methods of an interface are abstract. They are fully declared including their parameter interface, but not implemented in the interface. All the classes that want to use an interface must implement all the methods of the interface. Otherwise, the class becomes an abstract class.

We use the following syntax in the implementation part of the class −

```
INTERFACE <intf_name>.
```

In this syntax, <intf_name> represents the name of an interface. Note that this syntax must be used in the public section of the class.

The following syntax is used to implement the methods of an interface inside the implementation of a class −

METHOD <intf_name~method_m>.
<statements>.
ENDMETHOD.

In this syntax, <intf_name~method_m> represents the fully declared name of a method of the <intf_name> interface.


## Example

Report ZINTERFACE1.
INTERFACE my_interface1.
Methods msg.
ENDINTERFACE.

CLASS num_counter Definition.
PUBLIC Section.
INTERFACES my_interface1.
Methods add_number.
PRIVATE Section.
Data num Type I.
ENDCLASS.

CLASS num_counter Implementation.
Method my_interface1~msg.
Write: / 'The number is', num.
EndMethod.

Method add_number.
ADD 7 TO num.
EndMethod.
ENDCLASS.

CLASS drive1 Definition.
PUBLIC Section.
INTERFACES my_interface1.
Methods speed1.
PRIVATE Section.
Data wheel1 Type I.
ENDCLASS.

CLASS drive1 Implementation.
Method my_interface1~msg.
Write: / 'Total number of wheels is', wheel1.
EndMethod.

```
Method speed1.
Add 4 To wheel1.
EndMethod.
ENDCLASS.

Start-Of-Selection.
Data object1 Type Ref To num_counter.
Create Object object1.

CALL Method object1→add_number.
CALL Method object1→my_interface1~msg.

Data object2 Type Ref To drive1.
Create Object object2.

CALL Method object2→speed1.
CALL Method object2→my_interface1~msg.
```

The above code produces the following output −

```
The number is 7
Total number of wheels is 4
```

In the above example, my_interface1 is the name of an interface that contains the 'msg' method. Next, two classes, num_counter and drive1 are defined and implemented. Both these classes implement the 'msg' method and also specific methods that define the behavior of their respective instances, such as the add_number and speed1 methods.

**Note** − The add_number and speed1 methods are specific to the respective classes.

# SAP ABAP - OBJECT EVENTS

An event is a set of outcomes that are defined in a class to trigger the event handlers in other classes. When an event is triggered, we can call any number of event handler methods. The link between a trigger and its handler method is actually decided dynamically at run-time.

In a normal method call, a calling program determines which method of an object or a class needs to be called. As fixed handler method is not registered for every event, in case of event handling, the handler method determines the event that needs to be triggered.

An event of a class can trigger an event handler method of the same class by using the RAISE EVENT statement. For an event, the event handler method can be defined in the same or different class by using the FOR EVENT clause, as shown in the following syntax −

---

FOR EVENT <event_name> OF <class_name>.

---

Similar to the methods of a class, an event can have parameter interface but it has only output parameters. The output parameters are passed to the event handler method by the RAISE EVENT statement that receives them as input parameters. An event is linked to its handler method dynamically in a program by using the SET HANDLER statement.

When an event is triggered, appropriate event handler methods are supposed to be executed in all the handling classes.


## Example

---

```
REPORT ZEVENT1.
CLASS CL_main DEFINITION.
PUBLIC SECTION.
DATA: num1 TYPE I.
METHODS: PRO IMPORTING num2 TYPE I.
EVENTS: CUTOFF.
ENDCLASS.

CLASS CL_eventhandler DEFINITION.
PUBLIC SECTION.
METHODS: handling_CUTOFF FOR EVENT CUTOFF OF CL_main.
ENDCLASS.
```

---

```
START-OF-SELECTION.
DATA: main1 TYPE REF TO CL_main.
DATA: eventhandler1 TYPE REF TO CL_eventhandler.

CREATE OBJECT main1.
CREATE OBJECT eventhandler1.

SET HANDLER eventhandler1→handling_CUTOFF FOR main1.
main1→PRO( 4 ).
CLASS CL_main IMPLEMENTATION.
METHOD PRO.
num1 = num2.
IF num2 ≥ 2.
RAISE EVENT CUTOFF.
ENDIF.
ENDMETHOD.
ENDCLASS.

CLASS CL_eventhandler IMPLEMENTATION.
METHOD handling_CUTOFF.
WRITE: 'Handling the CutOff'.
WRITE: / 'Event has been processed'.
ENDMETHOD. ENDCLASS.
```

The above code produces the following output −

```
Handling the CutOff
Event has been processed
```

# SAP ABAP - REPORT PROGRAMMING

A report is a presentation of data in an organized structure. Many database management systems include a report writer that enables you to design and generate reports. SAP applications support report creation.

A classical report is created by using the output data in the WRITE statement inside a loop. They do not contain any sub-reports. SAP also provides some standard reports such as RSCLTCOP that is used to copy tables across clients and RSPARAM that is used to display instance parameters.

These reports consist of only one screen as an output. We can use various events such as INITIALIZATON & TOP-OF-PAGE to create a classical report, and each event has its own importance during the creation of a classical report. Each of these events is associated to a specific user action and is triggered only when the user performs that action.

Following is a table describing the events and descriptions −

| S.No. | Event & Description |
| --- | --- |
| 1 | **INITIALIZATON**<br>Triggered before displaying the selection screen. |
| 2 | **AT SELECTION-SCREEN**<br>Triggered after processing of the user input on the selection screen. This event verifies the user input prior to the execution of a program. After processing the user input, the selection screen remains in the active mode. |
| 3 | **START-OF-SELECTION**<br>Triggered only after the processing of the selection screen is over; that is, when the user clicks the Execute icon on the selection screen. |
| 4 | **END-OF-SELECTION**<br>Triggered after the last statement in the START-OF-SELECTON event is executed. |
| 5 | **TOP-OF-PAGE**<br>Triggered by the first WRITE statement to display the data on a new page. |
| 6 | **END-OF-PAGE**<br>Triggered to display the text at the end of a page in a report. Note, that |

this event is the last event while creating a report, and should be combined with the LINE-COUNT clause of the REPORT statement.

## Example.

Let's create a classical report. We will display the information stored in the standard database MARA (contains general material data) by using a sequence of statements in ABAP editor.

```
REPORT ZREPORT2
LINE-SIZE 75
LINE-COUNT 30(3)
NO STANDARD PAGE HEADING.
Tables: MARA.
TYPES: Begin of itab,

MATNR TYPE MARA-MATNR,
MBRSH TYPE MARA-MBRSH,
MEINS TYPE MARA-MEINS,
MTART TYPE MARA-MTART,

End of itab.

DATA: wa_ma TYPE itab,
    it_ma TYPE STANDARD TABLE OF itab.

SELECT-OPTIONS: MATS FOR MARA-MATNR OBLIGATORY.
INITIALIZATION.
MATS-LOW = '1'.
MATS-HIGH = '500'.

APPEND MATS.
AT SELECTION-SCREEN. .
IF MATS-LOW = ' '.
MESSAGE I000(ZKMESSAGE).
ELSEIF MATS-HIGH = ' '.
MESSAGE I001(ZKMESSAGE).
ENDIF.

TOP-OF-PAGE.
WRITE:/ 'CLASSICAL REPORT CONTAINING GENERAL MATERIAL
DATA
FROM THE TABLE MARA' COLOR 7.
ULINE.
```

```
WRITE:/ 'MATERIAL' COLOR 1,

24 'INDUSTRY' COLOR 2,
38 'UNITS' COLOR 3,
53 'MATERIAL TYPE' COLOR 4.
ULINE.
END-OF-PAGE.

START-OF-SELECTION.
SELECT MATNR MBRSH MEINS MTART FROM MARA
INTO TABLE it_ma WHERE MATNR IN MATS.
LOOP AT it_ma into wa_ma.
WRITE:/ wa_ma-MATNR,

25 wa_ma-MBRSH,
40 wa_ma-MEINS,
55 wa_ma-MTART.
ENDLOOP.
END-OF-SELECTION.

ULINE.
WRITE:/ 'CLASSICAL REPORT HAS BEEN CREATED' COLOR 7.
ULINE.
SKIP.
```

The above code produces the following output containing the general material data
from the standard table MARA −

| MATERIAL | INDUSTRY | UNITS | MATERIAL TYPE |
|---|---|---|---|
| 23 | 1 | EA | ROH |
| 38 | M | PC | HALB |
| 43 | 1 | HR | HAWA |
| 58 | M | PC | HIBE |
| 59 | M | PC | HIBE |
| 68 | M | PC | FHMI |
| 78 | M | PC | DIEN |
| 88 | M | PC | FERT |
| 89 | M | PC | FERT |
| 98 | M | PC | HALB |
| 170 | M | PC | NLAG |
| 178 | M | PC | NLAG |
| 188 | M | PC | NLAG |
| 288 | M | PC | HALB |
| 358 | M | PC | HAWA |
| 359 | M | PC | HAWA |

CLASSICAL REPORT HAS BEEN CREATED

# SAP ABAP - DIALOG PROGRAMMING

Dialog programming deals with the development of multiple objects. All these objects are linked hierarchically to the main program and they are executed in a sequence. Dialog program development makes use of tools in the ABAP workbench. These are the same tools used in standard SAP application development.

Here are the main components of dialog programs −

- ❖ Screens
- ❖ Module pools
- ❖ Subroutines
- ❖ Menus
- ❖ Transactions

## The Toolset

| Central Component | Tool | Transaction |
|---|---|---|
| All Components | Object Browser | SE80<br>Tools > ABAP Workbench ><br>Object Browser |
| Screen | Screen Painter | SE51<br>Tools > ABAP Workbench ><br>Screen Painter |
| ABAP/4 Module Pool | ABAP/4 Editor | SE38<br>Tools > ABAP Workbench ><br>ABAP/4 Editor |
| Dictionary Objects (tables, fields, etc.) | ABAP/4 Dictionary | SE11<br>Tools > ABAP Workbench ><br>ABAP/4 Dictionary |
| Menu | Menu Painter | SE41<br>Tools > ABAP Workbench ><br>Menu Painter |
| Transaction | Maintain Transaction | SE93<br>Tools > ABAP Workbench ><br>Development ><br>Other Tools > Transactions |

Dialog programs should be developed by the object browser (transaction: SE80) so that all objects become linked to the main program without having to explicitly point each object. Advanced navigation techniques enhance the process of moving from one object to the other.

Screens are made up of screen attributes, screen layout, fields and flow logic. The module pool consists of modularized syntax that is placed inside include programs of the dialog program. These modules can be invoked by the flow logic, which is processed by the dialog processor.

## Creating a New Dialog Program

**Step 1** – Within the transaction SE80, select 'Program' from the dropdown and enter a Z name for your custom SAP program as 'ZSCREENEX'.

**Step 2** – Press Enter, choose 'With TOP INCL' and click the 'Yes' button.

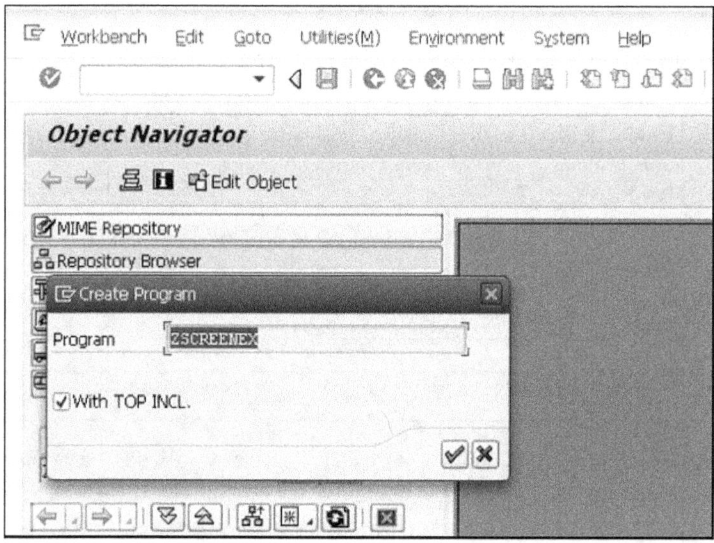

**Step 3** – Enter a name for your top include as 'ZSCRTOP' and click the green tick mark.

**Step 4** – Within the attributes screen, simply enter a title and click the save button.

## Adding a Screen to the Dialog Program

**Step 1** – To add a screen to the program, right-click on the program name and select the options Create → Screen.

**Step 2** – Enter a screen number as '0211' and click the green tick mark.

**Step 3** − In the next screen, enter a short title, set to normal screen type and click the save button on the top application toolbar.

## Screen Layout and Adding 'Hello World' Text

**Step 1** − Click the layout button within the application toolbar and the Screen Painter window appears.

**Step 2** − Add a Text Field and enter some text such as "Hello World".

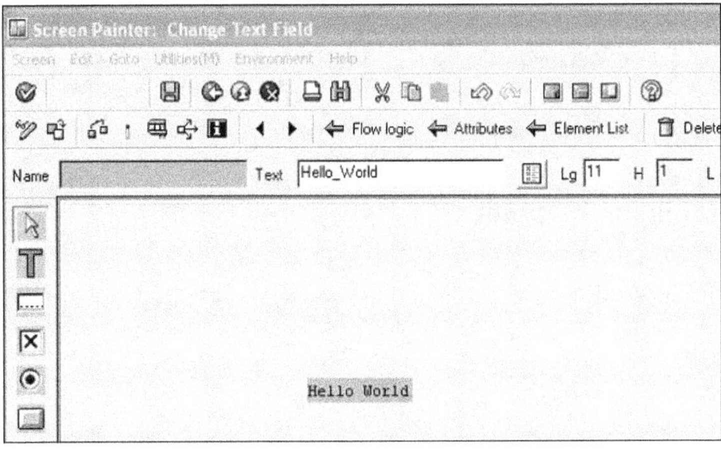


**Step 3** − Save and activate the screen.

## Creating Transaction

**Step 1** − To create a transaction code for your program, simply right click on the program name and choose the option Create → Transaction and enter a transaction code as 'ZTRANEX'.



**Step 2** − Enter the transaction text, program and screen you have just created (ZSCREENEX & 0211), and tick the 'SAPGUI for Windows' checkbox in the 'GUI support' section.

## Executing the Program

Save and activate everything. You can execute the program. As the program executes, the text you entered is displayed on the screen as shown in the following screenshot.

# SAP ABAP - SMART FORMS

SAP Smart Forms tool can be used to print and send documents. This tool is useful in developing forms, PDF files, e-mails and documents for the Internet. The tool provides an interface to build and maintain the layout and logic of a form. SAP also delivers a selection of forms for business processes such as those used in Customer Relationship Management (CRM), Sales and Distribution (SD), Financial Accounting (FI) and Human Resources (HR).

The tool allows you to modify forms by using simple graphical tools instead of using any programming tool. It means that a user with no programming knowledge can configure these forms with data for a business process effortlessly.

In a Smart Form, data is retrieved from static and dynamic tables. The table heading and subtotal are specified by the triggered events and the data is then sorted before the final output. A Smart Form allows you to incorporate graphics that can be displayed either as part of the form or as the background. You can also suppress a background graphic if required while taking a printout of a form.

Some examples of standard Smart Forms available in SAP system are as follows –

- ❖ SF_EXAMPLE_01 represents an invoice with a table output for flight booking for a customer.
- ❖ SF_EXAMPLE_02 represents an invoice similar to SF_EXAMPLE_01, but with subtotals.
- ❖ SF_EXAMPLE_03 specifies an invoice similar to SF_EXAMPLE_02, but one in which several customers can be selected in an application program.

## Creating a Form

Let's create a form by using the SAP Smart Forms tool. You will also learn how to add a node in the Smart Form and test the form in this tutorial. Here we begin with creating a copy of the SF_EXAMPLE_01 form. The SF_EXAMPLE_01 form is a standard Smart Form available in the SAP system.

**Step 1** – Smart Form Builder is the main interface used to build a Smart Form. It is available on the initial screen of SAP Smart Forms. We need to type the 'SMARTFORMS' transaction code in the Command field to open the initial screen of SAP Smart Forms. In this screen, enter the form name, SF_EXAMPLE_01, in the Form field.

**Step 2** – Select Smart Forms → Copy or click the Copy icon to open the Copy Form or Text dialog box.

**Step 3** − In the Target Object field, enter a name for the new form. The name must begin with the Y or Z letter. In this case, the name of the form is 'ZSMM1'.

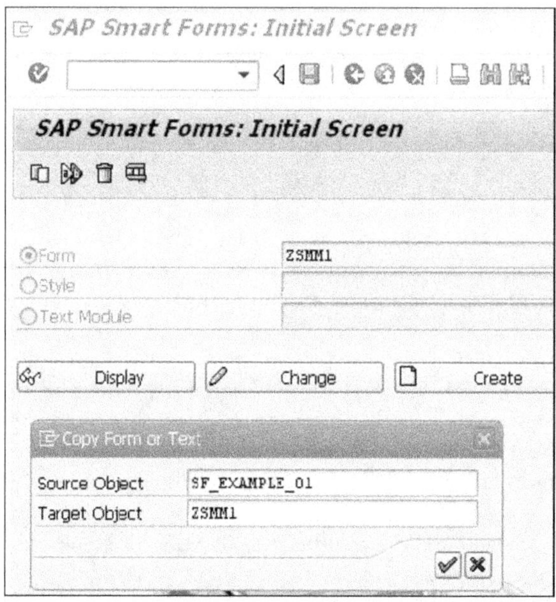

**Step 4** − Click the Continue icon or press the ENTER key in the Copy Form or Text dialog box so that the ZSMM1 form is created as a copy of the predefined form SF_EXAMPLE_01.

**Step 5** − Click the Save icon. The name of the form is displayed in the Form field on the initial screen of SAP Smart Forms.

**Step 6** − Click the Create button on the initial screen of SAP Smart Forms. The ZSMM1 form appears in Form Builder.

**Step 7** − The first draft page is created with a MAIN window. All the components of the new form are based on the SF_EXAMPLE_01 predefined form. You can just click a node in the Navigation menu to view its content.

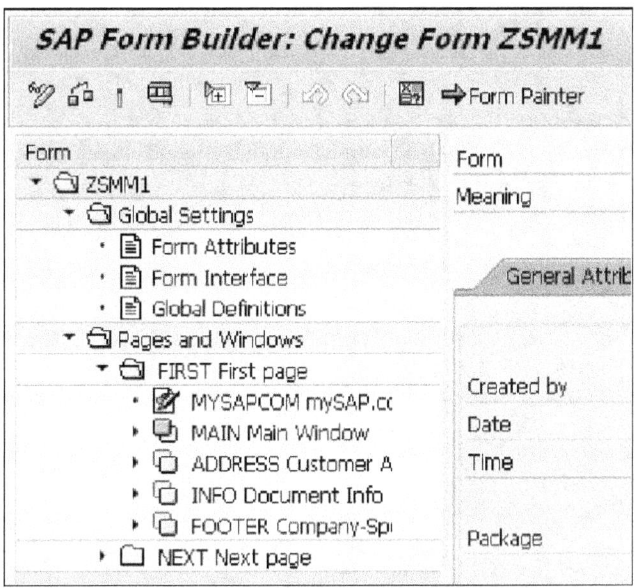


## Creating a Text Node in the Form

**Step 1** − Open a form in the change mode of the SAP Form Builder screen and right-click the Main Window option in the First Page node and select Create → Text from the context menu.

**Step 2** − Modify the text in the Text field to 'My_Text' and the text in the Meaning field to 'Text_Demo'. Enter the text 'Hello TutorialsPoint.....' in the text-editing box in the center frame of Form Builder as shown in the following snapshot −

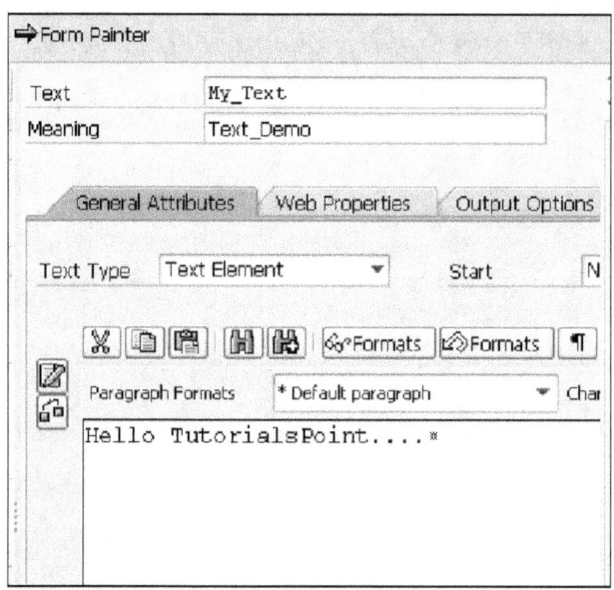


**Step 3** – Click the Save button to save the node.

**Step 4** – Activate and test the node by clicking the Activate and Test icons, respectively. The initial screen of Function Builder appears.

**Step 5** – Activate and test the function module by clicking the Activate and Execute icons. The parameters of the function module are displayed in the initial screen of Function Builder.

**Step 6** – Execute the function module by clicking the Execute icon. The Print dialog box appears.

**Step 7** – Specify the output device as 'LP01' and click the Print preview button.

The above steps will produce the following output –

IDES Holding Co. PO Box 9999, Sample City, xx9 9xx, United Kingdom

## Invoice

| | |
|---|---|
| Administrative clerk | Mr. Jones |
| Telephone | +1/2 12/99 10 99 |
| Telefax | +1/2 12/99 12 99 |
| Signed | 39999 / 2000 |
| Customer number | 00000000 |
| Date | 21.11.2015 |

Hello TutorialsPoint....
Dear Sir or Madam,

We would appreciate payment of the following invoice as soon
as possible. Thank you for placing your confidence in us.

| Carrier | Line | Flight Date | Departure | Price |
|---|---|---|---|---|
| Total | | | | |

Yours sincerely,
IDES HOLDING AG

# SAP ABAP - SAPSCRIPTS

The SAPscript tool of the SAP system can be used to build and manage business forms such as invoices and purchase orders. The SAPscript tool provides numerous templates that simplify the designing of a business form to a great extent.

The SAP system comes with standard SAPscript forms that are delivered with the SAP standard client (generally as client 000). Following are a few examples of standard SAPscript forms delivered with client 000 −

| S.No. | Form Name & Description |
|---|---|
| 1 | **RVORDER01**<br>Sales Order Confirmation Form |
| 2 | **RVDELNOTE**<br>Packing List |
| 3 | **RVINVOICE01**<br>Invoice |
| 4 | **MEDRUCK**<br>Purchase Order |
| 5 | **F110_PRENUM_CHCK**<br>Prenumbered Check |

The structure of a SAPscript form consists of 2 main components −

**Content** − This can be either text (business data) or graphics (company logo).

**Layout** − This is defined by a set of windows in which the form content appears.

## SAPscript − Form Painter Tool

The Form Painter tool provides the graphical layout of a SAPscript form and various functionalities to manipulate the form. In the following example, we are going to create an invoice form after copying its layout structure from a standard SAPscript form RVINVOICE01, and display its layout by accessing the Form Painter tool.

**Step 1** − Open the Form Painter. You may request the screen either by navigating the SAP menu or by using the SE71 transaction code.

**Step 2** − In the Form Painter, request screen, enter a name and language for a SAPscript form in the Form and Language fields, respectively. Let's enter 'RVINVOICE01' and 'EN' respectively in these fields.

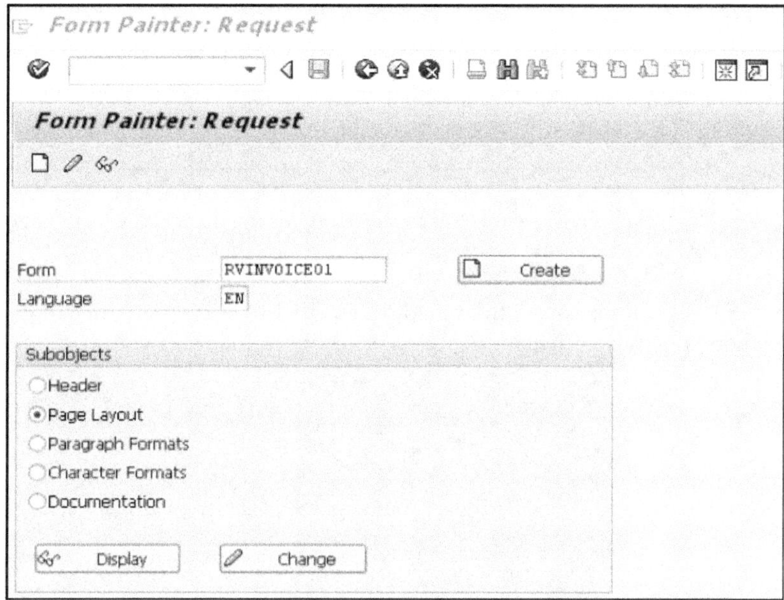

**Step 3** − Select the Page Layout radio button in the Sub objects group box.

**Step 4** − Select Utilities → Copy from Client to create a copy of the RVINVOICE01 form. The 'Copy Forms Between Clients' screen appears.

**Step 5** − In the 'Copy Forms Between Clients' screen, enter the original name of the form, 'RVINVOICE01', in the Form Name field, the number of the source client '000' in the Source Client field, and the name of the target form as 'ZINV_01' in the Target Form field. Make sure that other settings remain unchanged.

**Step 6** − Next, click the Execute icon in the 'Copy Forms Between Clients' screen. The 'Create Object Directory Entry' dialog box appears. Click the Save icon.

The ZINV_01 form is copied from the RVINVOICE01 form and displayed in the 'Copy Forms Between Clients screen' as depicted in the following snapshot −

```
Copy Forms Between Clients

Copy Forms Between Clients
________________________________________________________________

ZINV_01 : Original language set to D
ZINV_01 : Definition D copied
ZINV_01 : Language d copied
ZINV_01 : Language c copied
ZINV_01 : Language W copied
ZINV_01 : Language V copied
ZINV_01 : Language U copied
ZINV_01 : Language S copied
ZINV_01 : Language R copied
ZINV_01 : Language Q copied
ZINV_01 : Language P copied
ZINV_01 : Language O copied
ZINV_01 : Language N copied
ZINV_01 : Language M copied
ZINV_01 : Language L copied
ZINV_01 : Language K copied
ZINV_01 : Language J copied
ZINV_01 : Language I copied
ZINV_01 : Language H copied
ZINV_01 : Language F copied
ZINV_01 : Language E copied
ZINV_01 : Language D copied
ZINV_01 : Language C copied
ZINV_01 : Language B copied
ZINV_01 : Language 8 copied
ZINV_01 : Language 6 copied
ZINV_01 : Language 5 copied
ZINV_01 : Language 4 copied
ZINV_01 : Language 3 copied
ZINV_01 : Language 2 copied
ZINV_01 : Language 1 copied
```

**Step 7** − Click the back icon twice and navigate back to the Form Painter: Request screen, which contains the name of the copied form ZINV_01.

**Step 8** − After clicking the Display button, the 'Form ZINV_01: Layout of Page FIRST' window and the 'Form: Change Page Layout: ZINV_01' screen appears as shown in the following screenshot.

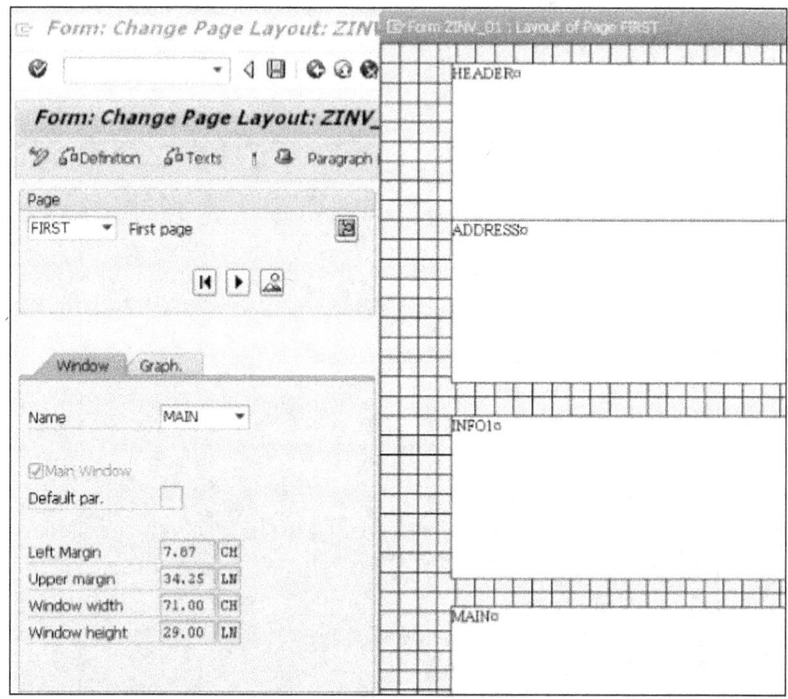


**Step 9** − The 'Form ZINV_01: Layout of Page FIRST' window shows the initial layout of the form. The layout of the form contains five windows: HEADER, ADDRESS, INFO, INFO1, and MAIN. The description of these windows can be accessed in PC Editor.

For instance, by just selecting the MAIN window and clicking the Text icon in the 'Form: Change Page Layout: ZINV_01' screen, you can view all the margin values as shown in the following screenshot −

# SAP ABAP - CUSTOMER EXITS

Customer exits could be considered as hooks to the SAP standard programs. We do not need an access key to write the code and there is no need to modify the SAP standard program. These exits don't have any functionality and they are empty. Business logic could be added in order to meet various client requirements. However, Customer Exits are not available for all programs.

## Customer Exits for Standard Transactions

Following are the steps to find customer exits as far as standard transactions are concerned. Let's identify customer exits available in MM01 (Material Master Creation).

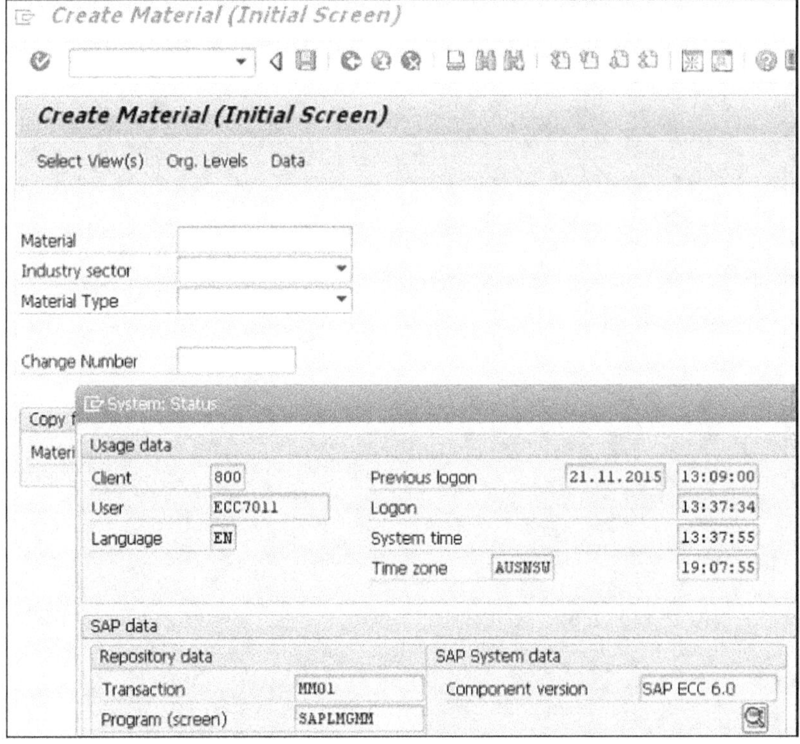

**Step 1** – Go to transaction MM01 and identify the program name of MM01 by going to Menu bar → System → Status as shown in the above screenshot.

**Step 2** – Get the program name from the popup screen. The program name is 'SAPLMGMM'.

**Step 3** – Go to transaction SE38, enter the program name and click Display.

**Step 4** – Navigate to Go to → Properties and find out the package of this program name.

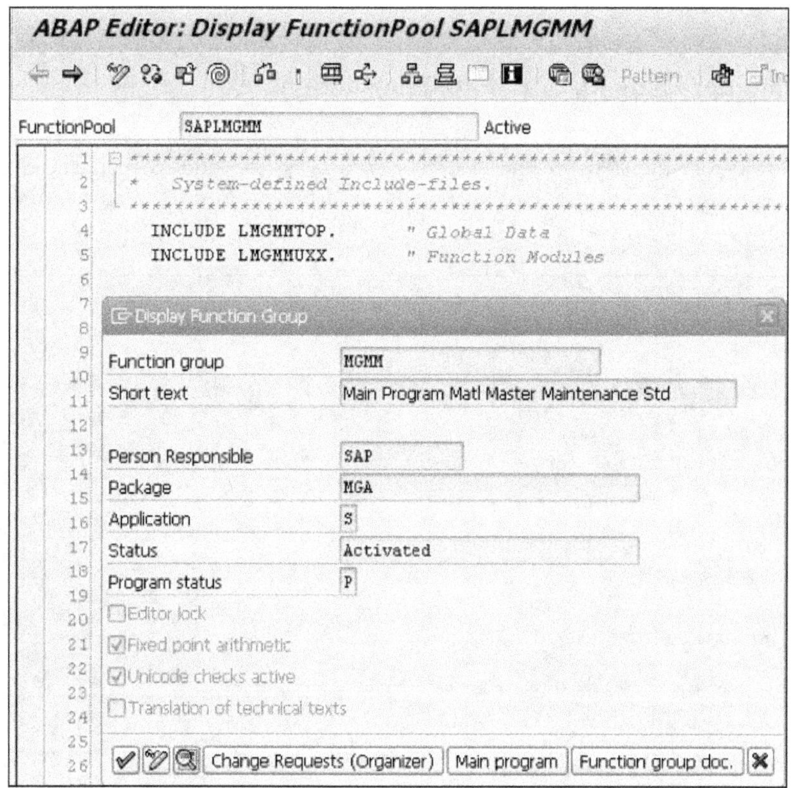

The package name is 'MGA'.

**Step 5** – Go to transaction code SMOD that is usually used to identify customer exits. Navigate to Utilities → Find (or) you may directly press Ctrl + F on the transaction code SMOD.

**Step 6** – After going to the 'Find Exits' screen, enter the package name we got earlier and press F8 (Execute) button.

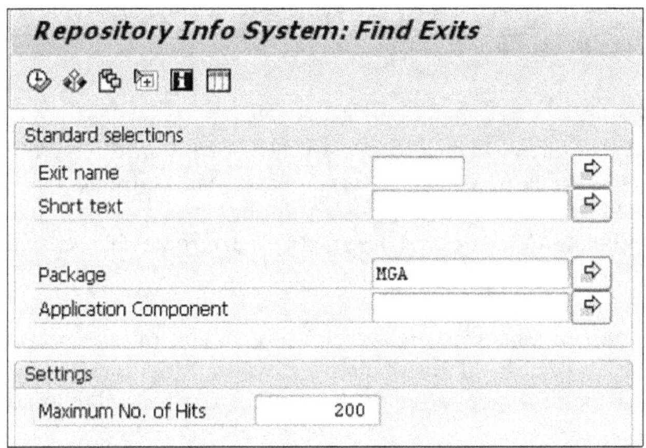

The above steps produce the following output with the list of exits available in the
Material Master Creation.

# SAP ABAP - USER EXITS

User exits are used in an extraction if the standard SAP extractors do not provide the expected data or the required functionality, for instance in authorizations or time checks. User exits are commonly used in Sales and Distribution (SD) modules. There are many exits provided by SAP in the areas of sales, transportation, shipping and billing. A user exit is designed to make some changes when standard SAP is not capable of fulfilling all the requirements.

To be able to access what exits are available in each area of sales, go to IMG using this path: IMG → Sales and Distribution → System Modifications → User Exits. The documentation for each exit in the areas of SD is explained thoroughly.

For instance, if you want to find user exits in Sales Document Processing (contract, quotation or sales order), follow the path mentioned above and continue to expand the node User Exits in Sales → User Exits. Click on icon documentation to see all user exits available in Sales Document Processing.

| S.No. | User Exit & Description |
|---|---|
| 1 | **USEREXIT_FIELD_MODIFICATION**<br>Used to modify screen attributes. |
| 2 | **USEREXIT_SAVE_DOCUMENT**<br>Helps in performing operations when the user hits Save. |
| 3 | **USEREXIT_SAVE_DOCUMENT_PREPARE**<br>Very useful to check input fields, put any value in the field or show a popup to users and to confirm the document. |
| 4 | **USEREXIT_MOVE_FIELD_TO_VBAK**<br>Used when user header changes are moved to header work area. |
| 5 | **USEREXIT_MOVE_FIELD_TO_VBAP**<br>Used when user item changes are moved to SAP item work area. |

A User Exit serves the same purpose as Customer Exits but they are available only for the SD module. The exit is implemented as a call to a Function Module. User Exits are modifications to SAP standard programs.

## Example

```
REPORT ZUSEREXIT1.
```

```abap
TABLES:
  TSTC, TSTCT,
  TADIR, TRDIR, TFDIR, ENLFDIR,
  MODSAPT, MODACT.

DATA:
  JTAB LIKE TADIR OCCURS 0 WITH HEADER LINE,
  field1(30),
  v_devclass LIKE TADIR-devclass.

PARAMETERS:
  P_TCODE LIKE TSTC-tcode OBLIGATORY.

SELECT SINGLE *
  FROM TSTC
  WHERE tcode EQ P_TCODE.

IF SY-SUBRC EQ 0.
  SELECT SINGLE *
  FROM TADIR

  WHERE pgmid = 'R3TR' AND
      object = 'PROG' AND
      obj_name = TSTC-pgmna.

  MOVE TADIR-devclass TO v_devclass.

  IF SY-SUBRC NE 0.
  SELECT SINGLE *
    FROM TRDIR
    WHERE name = TSTC-pgmna.

  IF TRDIR-subc EQ 'F'.
    SELECT SINGLE *
      FROM TFDIR
      WHERE pname = TSTC-pgmna.

    SELECT SINGLE *
      FROM ENLFDIR
      WHERE funcname = TFDIR-funcname.

    SELECT SINGLE *
      FROM TADIR
      WHERE pgmid = 'R3TR' AND
          object = 'FUGR' AND
          obj_name EQ ENLFDIR-area.
      MOVE TADIR-devclass TO v_devclass.
```

```abap
      ENDIF.
ENDIF.

SELECT *
  FROM TADIR
  INTO TABLE JTAB

    WHERE pgmid = 'R3TR' AND
      object = 'SMOD' AND
      devclass = v_devclass.

SELECT SINGLE *
  FROM TSTCT
  WHERE sprsl EQ SY-LANGU AND
     tcode EQ P_TCODE.

FORMAT COLOR COL_POSITIVE INTENSIFIED OFF.
WRITE:/(19) 'Transaction Code - ',
  20(20) P_TCODE,
  45(50) TSTCT-ttext.
SKIP.

IF NOT JTAB[] IS INITIAL.
   WRITE:/(95) SY-ULINE.
   FORMAT COLOR COL_HEADING INTENSIFIED ON.

   WRITE:/1 SY-VLINE,
       2 'Exit Name',
       21 SY-VLINE ,
       22 'Description',
       95 SY-VLINE.

   WRITE:/(95) SY-ULINE.
   LOOP AT JTAB.
     SELECT SINGLE * FROM MODSAPT
     WHERE sprsl = SY-LANGU AND
        name = JTAB-obj_name.

     FORMAT COLOR COL_NORMAL INTENSIFIED OFF.
     WRITE:/1 SY-VLINE,
         2 JTAB-obj_name HOTSPOT ON,
         21 SY-VLINE ,
         22 MODSAPT-modtext,
         95 SY-VLINE.
   ENDLOOP.

   WRITE:/(95) SY-ULINE.
```

```
  DESCRIBE TABLE JTAB.
  SKIP.
  FORMAT COLOR COL_TOTAL INTENSIFIED ON.
  WRITE:/ 'No of Exits:' , SY-TFILL.

 ELSE.
   FORMAT COLOR COL_NEGATIVE INTENSIFIED ON.
   WRITE:/(95) 'User Exit doesn't exist'.
 ENDIF.
ELSE.

 FORMAT COLOR COL_NEGATIVE INTENSIFIED ON.
 WRITE:/(95) 'Transaction Code Does Not Exist'.
ENDIF.

AT LINE-SELECTION.
  GET CURSOR FIELD field1.
  CHECK field1(4) EQ 'JTAB'.
  SET PARAMETER ID 'MON' FIELD sy-lisel+1(10).
  CALL TRANSACTION 'SMOD' AND SKIP FIRST SCREEN.
```

While processing, enter the transaction code 'ME01' and press F8 (Execute) button. The above code produces the following output −

# SAP ABAP - BUSINESS ADD-INS

In some cases, special functions need to be predefined in a software application to enhance the functionality of various applications. There are many Microsoft Excel add-ins to improve the functionality of MS Excel. Similarly, SAP facilitates some predefined functions by providing Business Add-Ins known as BADIs.

A BADI is an enhancement technique that facilitates a SAP programmer, a user, or a specific industry to add some additional code to the existing program in SAP system. We can use standard or customized logic to improve the SAP system. A BADI must first be defined and then implemented to enhance SAP application. While defining a BADI, an interface is created. BADI is implemented by this interface, which in turn is implemented by one or more adaptor classes.

The BADI technique is different from other enhancement techniques in two ways –

> ❖ Enhancement technique can be implemented only once.
> ❖ This enhancement technique can be used by many customers simultaneously.

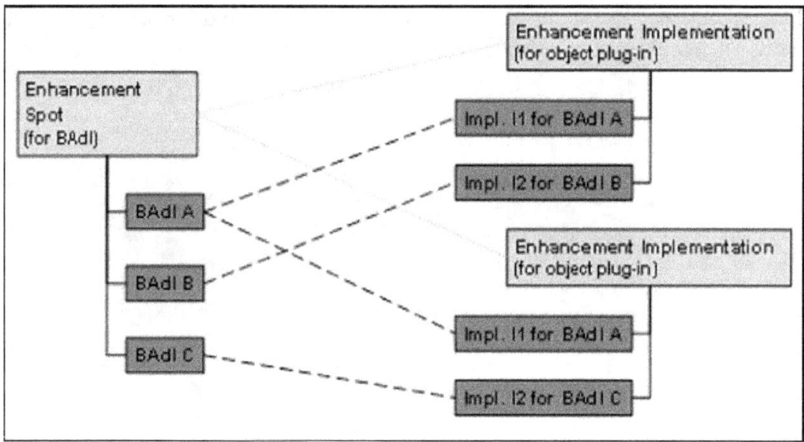


You can also create filter BADIs, which means BADIs are defined on the basis of filtered data that is not possible with enhancement techniques. The concept of BADIs has been redefined in SAP Release 7.0 with the following goals –

> ❖ Enhancing the standard applications in a SAP system by adding two new elements in the ABAP language, that is 'GET BADI' and 'CALL BADI'.
> ❖ Offering more flexibility features such as contexts and filters for the enhancement of standard applications in a SAP system.

When a BADI is created, it contains an interface and other additional components, such as function codes for menu enhancements and screen enhancements. A BADI creation allows customers to include their own enhancements in the standard SAP application. The enhancement, interface, and generated classes are located in an appropriate application development namespace.

Hence, a BADI can be considered as an enhancement technique that uses ABAP objects to create 'predefined points' in the SAP components. These predefined points are then implemented by individual industry solutions, country variants, partners and customers to suit their specific requirements. SAP actually introduced the BADI enhancement technique with the Release 4.6A, and the technique has been re-implemented again in the Release 7.0.

# SAP ABAP - WEB DYNPRO

Web Dynpro (WD) for ABAP is the SAP standard user interface technology developed by SAP AG. It can be used in the development of web-based applications in the SAP ABAP environment that utilizes SAP development tools and concepts. It provides a front-end web user interface to connect directly to backend SAP R/3 systems to access data and functions for reporting.

Web Dynpro for ABAP consists of a run-time environment and a graphical development environment with specific development tools that are integrated in the ABAP Workbench (transaction: SE80).

## Architecture of Web Dynpro

The following illustration shows the overall architecture of Web Dynpro −

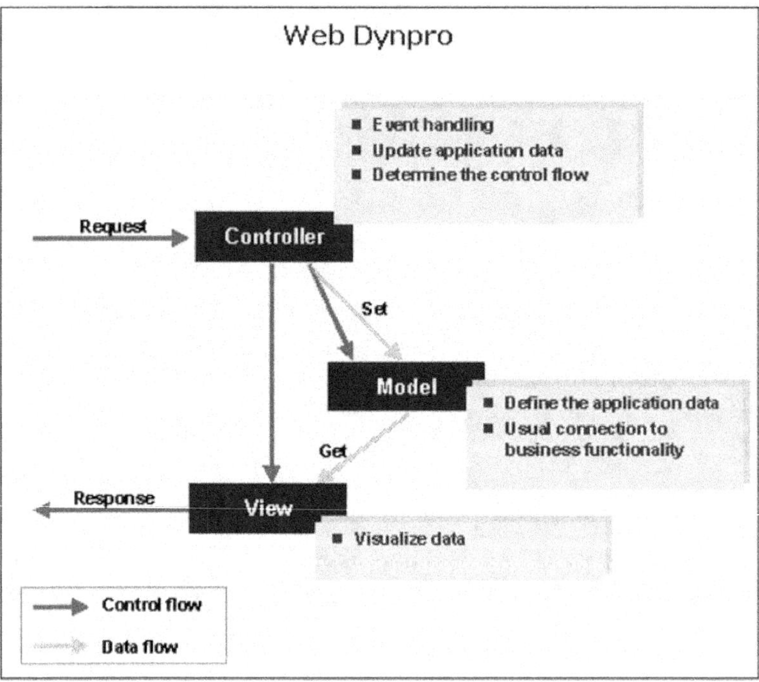


Following are a few points to keep in mind regarding Web Dynpro −

 ❖ Web Dynpro is the SAP NetWeaver programming model for user interfaces.

* ❖ All Web Dynpro applications are structured as per the Model View Controller (MVC) programming model.
* ❖ The model defines an interface to the main system and the Web Dynpro application can have an access to system data.
* ❖ The view is responsible for showing the data in the web browser.
* ❖ The controller resides between the view and the model. The controller formats the model data to be displayed in the view. It processes the user entries made by the user and returns them to the model.

## Advantages

Web Dynpro offers the following advantages for application developers −

* ❖ The use of graphical tools significantly reduces the implementation effort.
* ❖ Reuse and better maintainability by using components.
* ❖ The layout and navigation is easily changed using the Web Dynpro tools.
* ❖ User interface accessibility is supported.
* ❖ Full integration in the ABAP development environment.

## Web Dynpro Component and Window

The component is the global unit of the Web Dynpro application project. Creating a Web Dynpro component is the initial step in developing a new Web Dynpro application. Once the component is created, it acts as a node in the Web Dynpro object list. You may create any number of component views in a component and assemble them in any number of the corresponding Web Dynpro windows.

At least one Web Dynpro window is contained in each Web Dynpro component. The Web Dynpro window embeds all the views that are displayed within the front-end web application. The window is processed in the window editors of the ABAP Workbench.

**Note**

* ❖ The component view displays all the administrative details for the application including the description, the name of the person who created it, the creation date, and the assigned development package.
* ❖ The Web Dynpro application is the independent object in the object list of the ABAP Workbench. The interaction between the window and the application is created by the interface view of a given window.

9 7 9 8 6 9 6 4 7 0 9 7 9